Lena River

Yakutsk

Petropaylovsk

S.   R.

Nikolaevsk

SAKHALIN

BAIKAL AMUR MAGISTRAL RY.

ara River

Skovorodino

Komsomolsk

Nizhneudinsk

Mogocha

Sovetskaya
Gavan

Lake Baikal

Amur River

Cheremkhovo

Chita

Khabarovsk

Irkutsk

Ulan Ude

CHINESE EASTERN RY.

Birobidzhan

Kizil Khoto
(TANNU TUVA)

Ulan Bator

Harbin

Voroshilov

MANCHURIA

Vladivostok

MONGOLIAN PEOPLES
REPUBLIC

Mukden

KOREA

C H I N A

Kalgan

Peiping

Port Arthur

Tsingtao

Yenan

JAPAN

Nanking

TIBET

Shanghai

Chungking

FORMOSA

tta

Through Russia's Back Door

·

RICHARD E. LAUTERBACH

Author of "These Are the Russians"

HARPER & BROTHERS PUBLISHERS

New York and London

This book is for

GRACE M. KRONTHAL

Contents

PREFACE   ix

Part I: THE VOYAGE OF THE *SMOLNY*
Shanghai to Vladivostok   1

Part II: AMERICANS IN SIBERIA
Vladivostok   31

Part III: 5,800 MILES ON THE TRANS-SIBERIAN
A. Vladivostok to Irkutsk   59
B. Irkutsk to Moscow   110

Part IV: THE WEARY ARE WARY
Moscow   147

Part V: MAJOR SOKOLOV SOUNDS OFF
Moscow to Berlin   182

Part VI: THE DWINDLING PEACE   195

Part VII: APPENDIX: AS IT SEEMS TO MOSCOW
A. Struggle of the Democratic Forces for the Final Defeat of
Fascism   220
B. The Lessons of the War   228
C. Stalin's Replies to Werth   235

PHOTOGRAPHIC ALBUM: PEOPLE AND PLACES   opp. 112

Acknowledgments

THE author's grateful acknowledgment is made: to the editors of *Life* for their sponsorship of the Siberian assignment and for permission to use the resulting text and photographic material in this book; all points of view in this book are my own and not necessarily those of my colleagues on *Life*; to Alice Weigel for technical assistance in the preparation of the manuscript; to Anthony Sodaro for the end-page map; to Frank Stockman for his aid in preparing the photographic section; and especially to Bettina Lauterbach.

Preface

THIS little book does not have the burden of being definitive about anything. It is just a narrow frame around the biggest and most baffling picture in the American mind today. The frame is one reporter's trip through Russia, a sound track of what the Russian people said to me on that journey and my hopes for more than World War III. This is by no means the last word on Russia or the Russians. It does not pretend to have "all the facts."

In America today we are becoming less and less tolerant of a balanced judgment on the Soviet Union. During the war we felt differently. Except for the diehards we were agreeably broadminded. After all, Russians were being killed fighting our common enemy.

To be a patriot in many groups today you can still profess admiration for the "Russian people," but you must categorically castigate *every* action of the Russian government and its leaders and cheer the State and War Departments' "get tough" line. In a few places where Russia is not considered a daily international menace you must also abandon reasonable balance and publicly declare that the Soviet Union is a Utopia, that the Soviet Union can do no wrong.

The Russia-can-do-no-wrong people will say, "Why do you

mention concentration camps?" I say, "It's true." They say, "Even if it is, why give more ammunition to those who hate Russian and want war?"

The let's-drop-the-bomb-now crowd will say, "Why do you quote all those Russians on the atom bomb without pointing out that they are all liars and if not liars just repeating propaganda? And would Russia have given us the bomb if she had it first?" Others will ask: "Why don't you mention how many millions there are in the concentration camps?"

I don't know. Neither do any Americans who claim they do.

Neither side will accept this book as "objective" and I do not blame them. An "objective" reporter to most Americans is one whose opinions agree with their own.

A reporter presenting his material goes through the process of selection. How important is the fact that a stateroom is seven feet long and five feet wide? I have not consciously omitted any important fact or any germane conversation because I thought it would swing a reader's opinion one way or the other. In the final chapter I have selected certain arguments to make a case for my own beliefs; there are hundreds of other arguments about how we can or cannot get along with Russia. I have set forth those which I consider the most important.

The reader is entitled to an explanation of how I managed to get into Siberia in the first place. At the conclusion of an assignment in Japan and China, I thought I'd try to return home via the Soviet Union. I did not really think it would be possible.

The Soviet Ambassador to China, Apollon Alexandrovich

PREFACE

Petrov, was chief of the Foreign Office press department while I was in Moscow as a correspondent during 1943 and 1944. In writing about my experiences in the Soviet Union, I called Petrov several uncomplimentary names. Fortunately last spring in Chungking when I went to apply for a visa Petrov had not seen my book. He had read only a favorable review in a Shanghai Russian newspaper. To my surprise he greeted me as an old friend, fondly recalled other correspondents with whom he had bickered and fought in Moscow. I said what about a transit visa. He said, "Certainly." I said, "You will have to ask Moscow first." He denied this. I said, "Look, Mr. Petrov, I have been in your country twice before. I know how such things work. You will have to ask Moscow first." Petrov called me on that and offered to write me out a visa on the spot—so long as it was a transit visa and not a regular one.

"Where would you like to enter our country?" he asked.

I suggested Alma Ata in Central Asia, since I had been there previously.

"Why not Vladivostok?" the Ambassador wanted to know.

I had not suggested Vladivostok because no correspondent had been there in many years—certainly not since 1940. I thought it might be considered a special military area. But when Petrov mentioned Vladivostok, I agreed.

The Ambassador was pleased to be quits of the Press Department assignment. He found his post in China much easier, much more pleasant. I found him more gracious and helpful than he had been in Moscow.

There was the usual delay in actually getting the visa when

PREFACE

I was ready to go. I do not know if Petrov checked with Moscow or not. With the help of the Soviet assistant military attaché in Shanghai, I booked and paid one hundred and fifty dollars for a passage on the Soviet motor ship, *Smolny.* Except for the incidents set down in the pages which follow, I was not checked on, interfered with, spied upon, coerced, guided, or restricted. I did not have the freedoms I would have had in the United States, but neither did I expect them.

A word about the photographs: if there are no beautiful pictures of Soviet art galleries to relieve the monotony of bleak Siberia, it is because getting permission to make such pictures might have taken months. I took the pictures I could take without asking permission and without going out of my way to ask for trouble. Considering these limitations, plus those of time and technique, I believe the photographs included in this book are honestly representative.

This account has been compiled mainly from my day-to-day notes. The trip, the people I talked with, the papers I read, helped me to understand the problem of Russia and the Russians better than I had previously. I have written this book in the hope that it may help others to understand the problem.

THROUGH RUSSIA'S BACK DOOR

PART I

THE VOYAGE OF THE *SMOLNY*
Shanghai to Vladivostok

THE *Smolny* stood out in the middle of the crowded Whang-poo River surrounded by Chinese junks, American warships and Yangtze river boats. I stood on the wharf surrounded by my luggage, wondering how to get out to the *Smolny*. A raggedly dressed coolie poling along in a flimsy sampan shouted up at me from the water, "Hey, Joe, boat you wanchee?" I didn't reply immediately, debating in my mind whether or not the sampan could hold me and all my gear. A foreigner's indecision is an open door for a Chinese trying to sell anything, whether it be a White Russian girl or a Parker 51 fountain pen and pencil set. The sampan scooted along the Whangpoo and stopped below the wharf where I was still hesitating.

"Okay, Joe," said the coolie, "you say which ship ten dollars American."

The outrageous price brought the desired results. "Three," I answered involuntarily. "That ship out there." I pointed.

"Okay," said the coolie, and he held up eight fingers.

"Three," I repeated, "take the bags."

A small boy appeared from nowhere and began to lower my luggage into the sampan. The coolie put the flight bag down and raised six fingers. "Very fine sampan," he sang, "master very safe." He grinned and blew his nose into the water.

"Five dollars," I said with a note of hopeful finality.

"Okay, Joe."

We made the trip, the sampan and my heart teetering all the way.

I was the first passenger aboard the *Smolny*. The second mate showed me to my cabin. It was on the upper deck, small, clean and bright, with an outside porthole, two metal beds, a chair, desk, closet and washstand. "Which bed?" I asked in Russian.

"Either one," replied the mate, "the whole cabin is yours."

Lieutenant Colonel Stepan Andreyev, the Soviet assistant military attaché, had instructed me to report on the ship at 9 A.M. The *Smolny* didn't sail until two in the afternoon. When I complained of this to Andreyev he winked and said in English, "Maybe it is because writers are notoriously unreliable people. I want to be sure you make the boat on time." He wore a spotless white uniform to see me off.

"You go home now through my country. I would like to go home through your country. Will you help me arrange this?" he asked.

I said I'd be delighted but that I had no official status. "Just ask for a visa," I advised, "and if it's all right with your government it will probably be all right with mine."

"All right," he said, "I will see you in New York or Washington."

"Fine."

"In meantime, please give my greetings to Moscow and if you write anything about my country please send me a copy."

"Even if it is unfavorable?"

He thought that was a fine joke. "Yes, of course," he laughed. Then he added anxiously, "But you like my country?"

"Yes, I like it," I said. He held out his hand. "You write what you see," he said quietly, "you are honest. But if you don't like something, try to remember we are still very young and try to understand reasons."

There was nobody around to carry baggage, so I lugged my stuff up to my cabin. Having installed myself, I went on deck to watch the loading. The ship's chief cargo seemed to be children ranging in age from four to fourteen. I learned there were fifty-nine of them, Shanghai Russians, many orphaned. They were being transported to the Soviet Union to enter children's homes, where they would become wards of the state.* A Tass correspondent who had come aboard to make some pictures told me, "A Chinese official came to my office and demanded, 'Why is your country taking these children

---

* By decree of the Presidium of the Supreme Soviet in 1946, Russians (who had been Russian nationals in 1917) were permitted to apply for Soviet citizenship. Most Shanghai Russians asked for and received Soviet passports but were not necessarily allowed to return to the U.S.S.R.

away from Shanghai?' I looked at him and said, 'Do you think it's better to leave the boys to become thieves and the girls to enter bawdy houses?' "

The children carried nothing of China with them except the familiar indigo blue of their cotton overalls. The local Soviet Club in Shanghai had bought them clothes and candies for the trip. One boy still clutched a tennis racquet, another a string of bananas; a girl cuddled a Shirley Temple doll in her arms. A wave of weeping swept the deck when the loud-speaker announced that mothers and fathers must leave. A lacquered blonde lady wearing nylon stockings and spiked heels cried bitterly over a four-year-old girl with black ringlets. "She's Russian but she's bad," the Tass man said, pointing to the high-heeled lady. "She works in a house, you know. This is the only way of saving her child. . . ."

Including the Chinese

About midday the dinner bell sounded. Anxious to meet as many people as possible, I seated myself at the largest table in the dining room. Almost everyone else in first-class was traveling with their families and the big communal table was ignored in favor of smaller tables for four or five. Finally the waiter seated two very large Chinese families at the table with me. This led to a rather strained relationship as there were eleven Chinese at the table and none of them spoke English. Only one of the Chinese spoke Russian, and his accent made him almost impossible to understand. At the next meal— again in the interests of sociability—I went to sit at a smaller table. The waiter intercepted me and led me back to the big table. "*This* is *your* place," he stated. He saw my unhappy look and tried to joke, "You are the chairman, you sit at the head."

After dinner when the Chinese immigration officials came aboard, they sent for me. The youthful officer in charge was glad to see me. "I do not speak Russian," he said, "it is nice to speak English. Have you exit visa?" I gave him my passport. There was no exit visa. "This is irregular," he said.

"I have no entry visa either," I replied, "that is also irregular."

The official conferred with his two non-English-speaking colleagues for a moment, then said: "If a man has no entry visa you cannot expect him to have exit visa. You are passed." We shook hands.

At 2:15 "Anchors Aweigh" blasted from the ship's loudspeakers and the *Smolny* weaved through the cluttered Whangpoo like a slightly drunken open field runner. As we passed the the Soviet consulate I saw the entire Russian staff had gathered on a balcony to cheer and wave. Persons unknown were frantically flapping a large white sheet from the window of *Time's* apartment on the sixteenth floor of the Broadway Mansions where I had lived. Joyously I waved a small handkerchief. A Russian woman, observing this interchange, smirked and remarked in Russian to her companion, "Poor boy. He doesn't realize it's only somebody shaking bread crumbs from a tablecloth."

We sailed to the mouth of the Yangtze and anchored for the night.

The *Smolny*, I discovered, was a motor ship of about 6,000 tons. It was commissioned in Leningrad in 1928 for the Baltic State Line, which plied between Leningrad, Hamburg and London. The ship achieved its greatest notoriety during the United Nations conference in 1945 when it was anchored in San Francisco Harbor supposedly laden down with champagne, vodka and caviar. Actually it served chiefly as a communications ship for Molotov & Company. The *Smolny* still had a fine radio shack completely equipped with the latest American apparatus.

The ship's library was fascinating. There were books in a half dozen languages including Hebrew. Most of them were in German and English. The heavy stuff included Lenin and Stalin and Marx and of course the record of the Trotsky treason trials in most languages. The English selection was catholic to say the least: *Leaves of Grass; The Disinherited*, a proletarian novel by Jack Conroy; *The Heir of Redclyffe*, by Charlotte M. Yonge; *The Backslider*, by Grant Allan; Engels on *The Housing Question; The Voice of the People*, by Glasgow; four volumes of Hazlitt's *Shakespeare*; Milton's *Complete Poetical Works; The Girls of St. Wodes*, by Meade; *To Have and to Hold;* and Fielding's *Tom Jones*.

Breakfast at seven thirty and consisted of bread, oleomargarine and tea. After breakfast I took a nap. When I woke up I overheard two men chiseling away old paint outside my porthole. "America must be an amazing place," said one in Russian. "Of course, without question," said the other.

"Everything is wonderful and right, nothing is wrong or bad," said the first.

6

"Would you like to be in America?" asked the second.

"Oh, no, I am sometimes both bad and wrong," said the first.

I tumbled out of my berth and they moved away, laughing.

Black Bread and Nausea

The sea was not very rough, but the ship had no heavy cargo to hold it down and it acted a little lightheaded. At late supper the first full day out only about a third of the passengers managed to reach the dining room.

On the third day there were slices of cold, raw fish for breakfast and although my stomach had not been queasy, I passed this up. Dinner at noon consisted of borscht, cabbage stew, black bread and one banana. No tea. This mess, I thought, was retribution for all the Soviet banquets I had attended and all the wisecracks I had made about the Russians being lavish with food to impress foreigners. At five they served the same borscht, a soggy fritter filled with particles of meat, and sweetened tea. The Chinese were completely amazed at the food and they ate much less than I did, which was probably one reason they continually felt so nauseated. One of the Chinese gentlemen was going with his family to Vladivostok as China's consul-general and the other to Tashkent, Uzbekistan, in a similar post.

Late supper, at seven thirty, was simple: bread and tea. This day the radio announced the death of the former Soviet president, Mikhail Ivanovich Kalinin.

After supper the ship slowed and stopped. "We are going

7

to stand the night," a crew member explained. "There are islands ahead and it is very dangerous." We stood.

The fourth day was very bright and warm. I went up on the captain's deck to peer at Japan through his American Lend-Lease field glasses. I could make out several half-sunken hulls between the islands.

The Shanghai children, who felt a little strange and a little sick the first few days, had by now completely taken over the ship. The first day out I remembered watching two small boys fist-fighting. An elder boy pulled them apart. "Don't you want to learn discipline like a Soviet?" he asked. The boys looked bewildered but ceased squabbling for five minutes. Now the boys had organized into gangs. Crew members made mock rifles for them out of wooden boards and the ex-Shanghailanders' chief occupation from dawn to dusk was war: maneuver, ambush attack, counterattack, raid, siege. Their enemies were all Japs. The familiar Soviet epithets "Fascist beast" and "German bandits" were not heard in their play.

The girls were different. They didn't roam as much. Occasionally they played "Ring-a-Round-a-Rosie" or "Farmer-in-the-Dell" on the forward deck, and I thought them quite well-behaved. When they sang they raised their voices in English, and the first time I heard them let go with "The Monkeys Have no Tails in Zamboanga" I literally fell off my chair. In their repertoire they also had *Bell Bottom Trousers* and *You Are My Sunshine*. The latter song, for some reason which history may detail, is known by all geishas in Japan and keesang in Korea and singsong girls in China. The Shanghai girls, old beyond their years, shed their indigo blue cotton overalls and began to appear in bizarre and startling hand-me-downs from mother: high heels, black lace gowns, tight-fitting sweaters.

A girl named Valya was coquettish. Someone told her to stop. "You are only fourteen," Valya was admonished. "No, fourteen-and-a-half," Valya pouted, smoothing her frock, "and besides my Chinese age is sixteen."

At sundown a big-eyed, pallid-cheeked ten-year-old girl suddenly felt homesick and started to sob. I tried to comfort her. "Daddy, daddy, I want my daddy," cried the little girl. I assured her that her daddy would be along on the very next ship. Gradually the child quieted down. I led her by the hand and pointed to the lower deck, saying, "See how nicely the others are playing?" Some of the other girls looked up. The pale little girl wrenched her hand away from me and scampered down the ladder to join the other girls, screaming impolite epithets at them.

The Three Blocs

It may not have been by design but the first-class passengers split into three separate and distinct blocs. First, the old-time or regular Soviet citizens—consular, trade and embassy employees returning to the Soviet Union. Second, the new Soviet citizens—Russian immigrants (Whites) who had recently acquired citizenship papers and who were going home, some of them for the first time. Third, the foreigners—me and the Chinese. The three groups rarely mixed. They ate at different tables. Their children, if any, did not play together.

I managed a few words with each group, but for the first few days our relations would hardly have been termed chummy. The captain, incidentally, ate alone with a man in a brown suit who resembled a cross between Jerry Colonna and Earl Browder.

Every effort was made to avoid political discussions. Once a new Soviet citizen asked me what I thought would happen in China if the government and the Communists had an all-out fight. I said it depended largely on external factors.

"That's right," he agreed. "If the Americans would leave, the Kuomintang would collapse in fifteen minutes."

"Why fifteen minutes?" I asked.

"Maybe an hour," the Russian was willing to concede, "Just time enough to go to their banks and draw out their money and get a ticket to Hongkong or Honolulu or Chicago." He wouldn't elaborate further.

My only other political talk the first few days was even briefer. An "old" Soviet citizen—a young girl who had been a receptionist in the Russian Embassy at Chungking—asked me how I had obtained permission to travel on the *Smolny*. I explained and asked if she were surprised.

"No, not while relations with America are good," she said.

This surprised me somewhat. "Are they good?" I asked innocently. If they were, I was surprised and delighted to hear about it.

Her blue eyes flickered. "Well, they should be," she said cryptically. And then she walked away.

At noon the radio was switched on. "*Govorit Vladivostok,*" droned the announcer, "Here is the latest news." The latest news included these items: that a technical workers' congress had resolved to improve methods of factory work; that a collective farm had delivered wheat above its quota for the month of May; that an expedition of architects had arrived in Tashkent to study ancient Uzbek culture so as to incorporate it in plans for new buildings in Tashkent. The sole exception to fifteen minutes of domestic news: a brief mention of new demands by the local autonomy movement in the Iranian province of Azerbaidzhan.

Then followed fifteen minutes devoted to a biographical sketch of Kalinin. Almost all day the radio was filled with encomiums about him, including lengthy statements from national and local leaders praising his contributions to the Union. After dinner I fell asleep over a book I had picked up in the library called *Sixty Letters about the Soviet Union* published in Moscow in 1936. The letters were from foreign workers, including Americans, who were then residents of the U.S.S.R., extolling the Soviet system.

Malinovsky or Tolbuchkin

The most interesting discovery I made on the fifth day was that one of the new Russians did not even speak Russian. He was studying a little book called *Hugo's Simplified System—How to Speak Simple Russian (New Orthography) in Three Months without a Master.* He called to someone and asked for a sentence using the word "me" in the dative case. His name was Peter and he spoke English with a British accent. He spoke German, too, but I wouldn't know with what kind of accent.

11

Toward dusk, four or five crew members gathered on the deck below me, telling stories. The lean, tattooed one called Nikolai, stripped to the waist, was recalling his army experiences. Except for the strangeness of the language and the names, the identical kind of talk could be going on in any American bar or barber shop or legion post meeting. Perhaps on a Great Lakes steamer. Nikolai's voice carried well. "It was outside Kishinev in '44," he was saying, "they suddenly counterattacked . . . me and my fellows had to hold a certain road. Malinovsky was on our southern flank—"

"Tolbuchkin," a sailor interrupted.

Nikolai went on grandly, "Malinovsky—*vso rovno*, he doesn't appear in the story one way or another. As I was saying. . . ."

"He wouldn't like that," the sailor objected.

"Who?"

"Tolbuchkin."

This brought loud guffaws. Nikolai lit a cigarette. "Malinovsky," he repeated. "As I was saying, we hadn't eaten except for the two slices of black bread I always kept in my greatcoat—"

"*That's* where the extra food always went," someone said.

"Quiet!" ordered Nikolai. "We heard rumblings of German tanks and we thought we were finished. . . ."

"Probably your stomachs!"

Nikolai ignored this. "Boris Alexandrovich—that's my friend who also comes from Rostov—said we should throw all our grenades at once. He said there was just one chance

12

the Fritzes would slow up, thinking we had greater forces and more ammunition than we actually had. . . ."

"You're wrong already," a heckler disagreed, "Germans don't think."

"Quiet! Well. We discussed it, the four of us. Nobody else had any plan so we accepted that of Boris. We had a dozen grenades or so and we threw them all at once and fell on our stomachs into holes."

"What happened?"

"Did they stop?"

"No, they opened fire—far over our heads. That was enough for Tolbuchkin's scouts to come and see what was up . . ."

"Malinovsky," said the sailor.

"All right," Nikolai grinned, "Malinovsky. As I said, they came and just in time, too. We captured four Mark V's that night. . . ."

"We?" the crowd laughed derisively. Nikolai threw his cigarette overboard and swung at the sailor. In a few seconds there was a free-for-all on the deck.

Occasionally there was music on the ship's radio, but most of the time after Kalinin's death the Soviet air waves were filled with his name. Editorials from newspapers were read, anecdotes recalled, speeches quoted. None of the passengers listened intently. They gave me the impression that Kalinin's passing from life had been anticipated once he had passed from his position as chairman of the Supreme Soviet's Presidium.

The pimply, tow-headed youth in the lavender polo shirt who operated the *Smolny's* radio shack had a fine assortment of American records. When I complimented him, he grinned and said, "I specialize in Spike Jones and his City Slickers. Have you heard them burlesque 'Cocktails for Two'?"

He played it for me and grinned all the way through it. Maybe, I thought, "Spike" Jones would be a better ambassador than "Beedle" Smith.

Poppa and Sonja Henie

By the fifth day on the ship I had a speaking relationship with at least a dozen passengers. There was a little boy of five named Johnny who shouted the first time he saw me wearing a khaki shirt, "Look, Mother, there is one G.I." His parents were an attractive young couple who had recently acquired Soviet citizenship. Johnny had been born and brought up in Shanghai during the war. He refused to speak any language but English although his parents were fluent in both Russian and German.

One pleasant old man called "Poppa" by his friends occasionally came out with strange recollections. During a discussion of Hollywood movies shown in Russia, Sonja Henie was mentioned.

"I skated with her in the Boston Garden," he recalled in English, "about 1937. I admired her very much then but I saw her last picture in Shanghai. I think it is called *It's a Pleasure*. Well, for me it was not. She did not do real figure skating, only a lot of tricks."

Poppa was reluctant to answer questions, but I finally pried

14

out of him that he had once been a figure skater himself and that he had entertained fans between the periods of professional hockey games in Boston. But he wouldn't say, at least not directly, why he was returning to Russia. A subsequent conversation made the reason easier to guess.

"Do you think the Russians will be permitted to enter the next Olympic games?" he asked me.

"It's not definite," I replied, "It must be decided whether Soviet athletes are paid or not."

Poppa was annoyed. "Of course they are paid. The government pays you if you are a turner or a welder or a skater. But that is the Soviet system. How else can a man make a living in Russia? There is no place for tennis bums and the like in the Soviet Union." He walked away from me, disgusted.

Talking with his wife later, I learned that Poppa could still cut a pretty figure on the ice although he was sixty. "He is a fine teacher, Poppa is," his wife boasted. "He may be able to help the Russians." They always spoke about the Russians in the third person although they, too, were Russians.

I asked one of Poppa's friends if the old man was going to coach Soviet skaters for the forthcoming Olympics. "They didn't give him a visa just so he could take a vacation in the Crimea," he snapped.

Fritz and the Push-Button War

Johnny's mother was charming. Her name was Anya and she was expecting another child within the month. She had

15

small fine features and a small-boned frame which set her apart from most of the Russian women aboard. I told her about my own children and complimented her on Johnny's good behavior. He obeyed beautifully.

"That's because he hasn't played with other children," she said. "Shanghai was so dirty we kept him indoors. Now in Russia he will be free to play outside."

"How long since you've been in Russia?" I asked Anya.

"Seven years," she sighed.

"Are you glad to be going back?"

"Certainly. There is a great difference between living in Russia and elsewhere which you probably cannot understand. Do you know in Russia I never knew what my friends were —as far as their race or creed was concerned? Now, I guess most of them were Jews just because living abroad has made me conscious of that."

Poppa, dressed in a gray glen plaid suit and a red sweater-vest, came and sat down on the bench next to us. Anya was knitting. Poppa lit a big cigar.

"How long is it since you've seen Moscow?" I asked Poppa. He didn't answer. I turned to Anya. "Why do you all dislike to answer questions?"

She laughed. "It's a reaction to living under the Japanese and Chinese. Always inspectors, always questionnaires. You have no idea."

"Life is worse now in Shanghai than when the Japs were there," said Poppa. "Prices are higher, job opportunities less. These shoes . . ." he pointed at his shiny new black shoes, "a

16

great bargain at forty dollars United States gold. In the States how much would they cost? Maybe four dollars, five maybe." He got up and walked away, saying, "I walk twenty times around the deck before every meal. Keeps my figure."

Anya told Johnny to stay away from the rail. He did so.

"Why do you speak nothing but English to Johnny?" I asked.

"Oh, he will pick up Russian once he's there. But I don't want him ever to lose his English. I had to study it. It will be natural for him."

"Your English is perfect. Quite American."

"We had a lot of your soldiers at our house in Shanghai," Anya said. "They liked to play with Johnny."

"What does your husband do?"

The lines around her pretty mouth set. "Ask him," she said. I could tell from her expression and her tone that she didn't think it was any of my business.

The last night aboard he told me himself. I had retired fairly early, but being unable to sleep I dressed and went up on deck. It was cold. I entered the salon. Anya was there knitting. Fritz, her husband, was reading. They invited me to sit down.

Fritz was much more Nordic than Slavic in appearance. He had thin, light hair, a long bony nose with small nostrils, hollow cheeks, a prominent, sharp chin and small, blue eyes. His hands were strong; his build slight but wiry.

Half-jokingly, I said, "Well, what do you think about the future of the world?"

Fritz carefully put aside his book, lit a cigarette, and began to answer my question seriously. "I think there cannot be a World War III," he said earnestly. He had a slight lisp. "Mankind must know this. I am a radio engineer. I know something of electronics, of atomic energy. The weapons used at the end of World War II are just a beginning, experiments. What you read in magazines about a push-button war is no exaggeration, believe me. I cannot conceive that statesmen, knowing this, can allow another war. If you mean by your question—and we cannot ignore it—specifically a war between the U.S.A. and the U.S.S.R., I cannot personally see what either people have to gain from it."

"Nor can I," I said.

Fritz went on, "The U.S.S.R. is trying to bring about friendly governments in all neighboring countries, using every means possible. It is said that you do not like the Soviet Union's methods. Probably the Soviet Union does not like the methods of some other countries. It is fine to talk and write of freedom and democracy, but it is written with machine guns in Indonesia and Greece. Britain is now the chief fermenter of trouble among the powers. She is in the place that France was after the last war—a second-rate power. So she is trying to save her crumbling empire by giving dominion status to her colonies and trying to bolster her prestige by playing the United States off against the U.S.S.R. in the Mediterranean and the Middle East."

"American liberals don't approve of Britain's conduct in Greece or Indonesia," I agreed, "they dislike it as much as they do Russia's in Iran."

Anya knitted, her fingers working like the well-oiled parts of machines. Fritz drew his nostrils together as he exhaled.

18

"You in America would understand the Iranian issue better if a hostile government came to power in Mexico and another great foreign power moved in on all the oil rights."

"Something like that happened during the reign of Napoleon," I said. I started to go on, but Fritz cut me off with an impatient gesture of his hand.

"But this business of securing borders and making sure of friendly neighbors is not so important for the next war. The United States will be in the range of Russian weapons, I can assure you, just as Russia will be within the range of yours whether Poland is friendly or not."

"Are you a Marxist?" I asked Fritz.

"What else?" He seemed surprised that there was an alternative. "Well, now, you ask about the future of the world. Economically? Our world cannot continue this way with periodic depressions and regular famines. It must be organized for life instead of death. I hope it can be done peacefully." He paused, put out his cigarette, and coughed. "In fact, it must be done peacefully because to do it any other way would mean the end. Oh, yes, there are always those 'optimists' who say there will be some people left after all wars to carry on our so-called civilization. I doubt it this time. Even so, it is small comfort."

"What's the solution?"

"The solution?" Fritz intertwined his long, bony fingers and cracked his knuckles. "The solution lies in the people. They must learn to understand each other and to understand what is to their interests. Statesmen can be wrong but in the long run the people must be right. Now there are so many lies, so much propaganda."

19

"I agree with you. But how can people get to know about each other when the press and other means of communication are restricted and controlled?"

Fritz had no answer. Anya said, "Your press in America seems just as controlled to us as ours does to you. Let me give an example. Could a correspondent, if he thought it was the truth, write continually favorable stories about the Chinese Communists and get them printed in the really big, mass circulation periodicals in America?"

I thought about it. "Probably not," I said, "unless he was someone with a big name like Quentin Reynolds. As a matter of fact, Edgar Snow has written favorable pieces about the Chinese Communists for the *Saturday Evening Post*."

"What about the New York *Times*?" Fritz demanded.

"No," I said, "it's unlikely. The publisher of the New York *Times* would probably decide, in all sincerity, that any correspondent of his who wrote continually favorable stories about the Chinese Communists was not a good reporter."

"Not good for the *Times*," Anya laughed.

"But," I said, "could a *Pravda* reporter write favorable stories about the Kuomintang?"

"Certainly not," said Fritz, "anybody who did would be a liar and a fool."

Anya heaved herself into standing position. "I think it's time for bed," she said sweetly, "and we have to pack."

The Golden Horn

Early in the morning of the sixth day land was sighted. The passengers, especially the children, were in a continual state of excitement. For the first time since we had left Shanghai the sun was completely hidden and the rocky islands along the Russian coast loomed deep purple in the soupy mist. The course into the harbor was a tortuous one through narrow channels.

I climbed up on the captain's bridge with my camera. The captain came over and admired my equipment.

"Have you ever been to Istanbul in Turkey?" he asked. I hadn't. "The famous harbor there is also 'Golden Horn.' In Russian, *Zolotoi Rog.*"

"How many months does Vladivostok Harbor freeze over?" I asked.

"From late December until the middle of April. We employ icebreakers. Your Liberty ships came here during the war."

The man in the brown suit who sat at the captain's table joined us on the bridge. "America sent over a hundred million dollars' worth of supplies to the Russian Army through here in the First World War," he said in Russian.

"Was Vladivostok bombed?" I asked.

"A few times, I think," said the captain. "It is about seven hundred miles from Tokyo. But only thirty-five miles from Manchuria and not much more from Korea."

About noon we could make out the city of Vladivostok. It is built on the side of a steep incline sweeping up from the harbor. The Golden Horn, the captain assured me, was one of the finest natural harbors in the world, completely protected by high shores. It is four miles long, a mile wide. The port facilities had been expanded many times during the war and some of the giant movable cranes which the captain pointed out had been shipped from the United States to expedite unloading of Lend-Lease supplies.

Now as the *Smolny* moved slowly towards the docks, the harbor seemed too peaceful. There were ships of all shapes and sizes, but the port was almost lifeless. At one pier a row of rusty-sided ex-Liberties were tied up. I asked the captain why these ships, all renamed after Soviet cities, were idle.

"Shortage of fuel oil," he said. "I have had to conserve."

In the berth adjacent to the one where we were heading was a Soviet transport, the *Dvina*, getting up steam. The ship's deck had the helter-skelter appearance of a Hollywood set after dismantling. It was laden down like Noah's Ark with almost everything: sailors, soldiers, engineers, women, children, nurses, livestock, trucks, jeeps, generators, crates of canned food and some munitions. As the *Smolny* was eased in alongside of her, I called over to a friendly looking sailor standing in the prow of the *Dvina*, "Where are you going?"

"That's a military secret," he yelled back, laughing. An army engineer standing next to the sailor cupped his hands and responded, "To Sakhalin Island to settle down for a bit."

I went below to the lower deck. A group of the new Soviet citizens were leaning over the rail appraising Vladivostok. They appeared disappointed. "I was here twenty years ago," observed Poppa, the figure skater. "I guess they haven't done very much with it."

"Boris Abramovich, you shouldn't talk like that," his wife scolded, "it might be very nice."

22

"Maybe," said Poppa, shaking his head. He turned to me. "How big is Vladivostok now?"

"About three hundred thousand," I said.

"You know it means Lord of the East—or Ruler of the East. The Russians came there in 1860. It was a free port until 1909 or 1910."

"Poppa has been reading Russian history," his wife said proudly.

Girls Never Make Passes

Valya and her ten-year-old friend, the lonely, homesick little girl who had cried, were standing near me. Valya, dressed again in the blue jeans, was talking loudly in Russian.

"You just go up to him and say in English like this, 'Mister, will you please take my picture and send it to my daddy?' Now say it, Ninotchka."

Ninotchka hid her head against Valya. Valya didn't look at me but repeated the sentence in English slowly. Ninotchka was still too shy. Valya sighed and said to me, "What can you do with a child like that?"

I told her I'd be very happy to take Ninotchka's picture and hers, too. "Where, when?" they both cried excitedly in Russian. I seated them near the rail and took a picture. Nina thanked me. Valya then sent her below to get her father's address and an envelope.

"What have you been doing?" I asked Valya.

"I was sick for a day or so," she said. "Then I've been going to the movies they show. All about Lenin and partisans.

I much prefer movies like *Sun Valley Serenade*. Do they have American movies in Russia?"

"Some." Then I asked her if she knew where she was going to stay in Vladivostok.

"I will stay near Vladivostok," she said. "The sick ones like Nina will go to the Ukraine, probably Kiev."

"Are you glad to be here?"

Valya needed no more urging to tell me the story of her life. She had been to French and English schools but she spoke Russian at home. Her father was a broker. She was an only child. During the war her parents had tried to go back to Russia and fight. Recently they had taken Soviet citizenship. They wanted Valya to become a good Russian so she was being sent away to a Russian school.

I asked her a few questions about Russia and about Communism. She seemed to know almost nothing about either. Then I asked her what she knew about Generalissimo Stalin.

"I can tell you more about the other one," she said.

"What other one?" I wondered if she meant Trotsky.

"The Chinese Gimo. Shanghai is full of gossip about him. But he doesn't interest me much. Neither does Stalin. Nor Truman nor Attlee."

Ninotchka came back and handed me the envelope and thanked me again.

"I won't ever marry *any* of them," Valya mused.

"Who?"

"Stalin, Chiang, Truman or Attlee. They all have awful moustaches except Truman and he wears glasses. I like you better. You haven't got either."

"Seditious Literature"

I went to my cabin and reloaded my camera. Shortly thereafter customs officials, wearing army uniforms with green bands around their hats, came aboard. With them came a dewy-eyed young blonde named Vera from Intourist, the agency which has to do with all travel by foreigners in the Soviet Union. Vera asked me whether I wished to stay at the American consulate. I explained emphatically that I had no connection with the United States Government or any of the armed forces and that I wanted to stay at a hotel. She looked unbelieving but promised to try and arrange it in an hour or so.

An official requested that I remain in my cabin until my luggage had been examined. The inspector decided, as a matter of protocol, to begin with me. Two men were assigned to the mission; the chief inspector, a smooth-shaven captain with almost no eyebrows, and a furtive young assistant who looked like a ferret.

Half-way through the painstaking inspection of my clothing, the dinner bell sounded. The captain in the green hat (he didn't take it off) suggested that I go and eat. I did. He closed the door of my cabin. When I had finished eating we resumed the inspection. He held up a large manila envelope.

"What's in here?" he asked in English.

"Don't bother with that," I said, "those are only pictures of me."

"Ah, yes," he said, half to himself, "and also two pony editions of the journal *Time*." He put the envelope down. I opened it. There *were* two old pony editions of *Time* which I had forgotten.

My flight bag containing clothing was finally checked. Next the captain opened the case which held my books, manuscripts, and typewriter. He took out nearly all the printed material and stacked it in a neat pile.

"These you cannot have," the green hat stated. In the pile were copies of Owen Lattimore's *Solution in Asia* (which was favorably reviewed in Moscow); General Marshall's *Report on the Army*; a pamphlet entitled *The United States and the United Nations*, a verbatim report on the San Francisco proceedings; an anthology, *Freedom Speaks*; four bound monographs on ancient Chinese cures, including *Treatment of Worm Diseases with Chinese Drugs*; and all my personal notebooks and letters, plus two manuscripts about China which had occupied part of my time aboard the ship.

"These I must take from you," said the green hat. "I will seal them in a package and give it to you and you cannot open it until you leave our country."

"It's against the spirit of the Soviet Union," I said, "You are taking stories away from me that I must work on. You are robbing a worker of his means of production."

That was a mistake. The green hat snapped quickly, "Oh no, I am not taking your typewriter."

We argued some more but he kept saying, "It's our law, I am sorry."

"What law?" I demanded. He pulled out a notebook and

read to me. It was a law pertaining to importation of "seditious literature."

I pointed to my Rolliflex which he had not yet seen. "I could understand it if you sealed up my camera. But why take my stories on China?"

"I am not interested in your camera," snapped the green hat, "you are free to use it."

I changed tactics. "Look, if I had come to the Soviet Union to flood it with counter-revolutionary propaganda, I'd be better prepared than this."

The green hat chewed that one over and rubbed his square chin thoughtfully. "Perhaps when you get to Moscow you can have an official open it there," he said tentatively.

"And lose the twelve days of work on the train?"

"It is our law," he repeated, "you will understand."

"No, I refuse to understand. What have a few sheets of typewritten paper got to do with your law on seditious literature? I will have to cable America about this."

The green hat said nothing but I thought he looked sheepish. His ferret-faced assistant was still fussing around. He pointed to an unopened case of army rations. "Open this!" he ordered. The green hat turned on him, "Don't bother with that, it's food, can't you see? And the seal isn't broken."

The ferret left the cabin and the green hat came close to me. "Here," he whispered, "here is your story on Chinese medicine. Put it away. I give you that. I understand you lose money." He shoved it at me. "Put it away," he repeated, "Everything is all right, yes?"

"Everything is all right *now*," I said, "but what happens

27

when the next Soviet official sees my camera? He may think
I brought it into the country illegally. Can't you give me a
paper or a document to show that it was passed?"

Green hat pondered. "I cannot give you a document to take
pictures," he said.

"All right. Just something to show that the camera and film
were not smuggled in."

"May I have your passport?" I gave it to him. He took out
a fountain pen and wrote in the back of my passport "professional equipment." Under that heading he listed, in Russian, the type and number of my camera and my typewriter.
He handed it back to me.

"Everything all right now?" he repeated formally in Russian.

"Everything all right," I said. We shook hands.

At this moment dewy-eyed Vera reappeared. "I have a room
for you in the hotel. Have you been through customs? Your
friends are waiting."

"What friends?"

Her eyes opened even wider. "Your friends. They are in
the salon. Didn't anybody tell you?"

I walked into the salon and there were four Americans,
grinning like cheerful apes. A navy commander, a lieutenant
commander and a chief petty officer in their dress blues
with all their ribbons, and a small, dark, bright-eyed girl.
I had never seen any of them before, but Vera had been
correct. They were friends.

"My God," said the commander, George Roullard, "you

are the first correspondent to pass through here in I don't know how long."

"It's wonderful," said the girl, "we know all about you."

The lieutenant commander introduced himself. He was the new naval attaché, Edward Ryan, a laconic blond youngster. Roullard, after several years in Vladivostok, was leaving. "You upset poor Smith," he said, referring to the United States vice-consul. "Intourist had a wire from the *Smolny* that an American was coming. Smith thought it was a State Department inspector coming to look over his books. He sat up nights making things balance."

"We thought you might be from the Seventh Fleet," the girl said. Her name was Irene and she worked for the naval attaché as a secretary and translator. "Everyone has been spitting on their brass."

"Then Vera, the Intourist girl, called us up a while ago and asked if we wanted you to stay at the consulate." The chief yeoman, Theodore Grason, said this. "We told her no."

"That's fine. I told her no, too."

"Vera's a good girl," said Roullard, "treat her right and the town is yours."

"If anyone wants it," said Ryan, "wait 'till you see it."

"Are you ready?" asked Grason. "I'll help you with your bags."

I said I thought I'd say goodbye to some of my friends aboard ship.

"You'd better," said Roullard. "You'll never see them again. Oh, you may see them, but they probably won't recognize you, and if they do they won't speak to you."

"As bad as that, eh?"

"Worse," said Grason, "let's get going."

"Did you bring any films? Any American movies?" Irene asked.

"Yes, they're on board," I said.

"Wonderful," said Irene. She took my arm.

"You'll get used to Irene," said Grason, "she's just been here too long. She's this way with every new man that comes along whether she knows anything about him or not."

"Shut up," said Irene, "he's a correspondent and he works for *Life*."

"Oh goody," Ryan said.

When I left the ship the Chinese consuls and the Russians, new Soviets and old citizens, were still struggling with customs. The returning Soviet Embassy officials had more difficulty than I did with the green hats. They were limited in the amount of new clothing which they could bring back to the Soviet Union: three suits, four pairs of shoes, so many shirts, socks, underwear, etc. Not only that. Most of them were forced to live aboard the *Smolny* until the next train left for Moscow, four days later. Vladivostok had few accommodations for transients other than foreigners or top drawer diplomats.

PART II

AMERICANS IN SIBERIA

Vladivostok

THE Americans drove me to my hotel in a new station wagon which seemed out of place among Vladivostok's ancient vehicles. Intourist, by law and by custom, unceremoniously evicted a Soviet citizen from a bed and I was installed in one of the finest rooms in the Chelyuskin. This hotel, a pre-revolutionary relic once known as the Versailles, had one toilet and one bathroom on every floor whether it was needed or not. The lobby of the hotel was dark and rather dirty. It could have been the entrance to a Third Avenue flophouse in New York. But the rest of the hotel was clean, the service proved to be excellent by any postwar standards, and the food —for me, at least—was far above average.

That first night, after I had bathed and changed, I walked up Tigerovaya Street to the American consulate, about a block from the hotel. Across the cobbled street from the consulate stood a sentinel, a member of the security police formerly called Cheka and then later NKVD. Behind him was a small wooden shack shaped like a telephone booth. When any of the Americans drove off in a car he was supposed to telephone a report to his headquarters so that a pursuer-on-wheels could set out behind the American vehicle.

The main gripe (and there were many) of the Americans in Vladivostok was their enforced isolation. Theoretically they were permitted the freedom of the city as far out as the road block at the Nineteenth Kilometer. Beyond this point, for reasons unknown, they could not venture without a special *propusk* which they had not yet been able to obtain. In such cases permission is never overtly refused; it is just not granted. The United States naval attaché had also requested permission to pay a courtesy visit to Soviet warships in the harbor. This routine request—that is, it is routine in other friendly countries—was also given the pigeonhole treatment.

All attempts by the United States colony to fraternize with the local population have also led to frustration. This is evidently not a postwar development engendered by growing suspicion of fear of America, but something that has persisted since the consulate was reopened in 1941 and which has its roots is tsarist times. The few Russian *devochkas* who were bold or curious enough to venture forth publicly accompanied by Americans were usually warned by Soviet officials. After one or two innocuous dates the frightened damsels begged the Americans to stay away. This rankled deep; it was not only a slap in the face to Soviet-American friendship but a body blow to the vanity of the American male who had seen and conquered throughout the world for the past five years.

According to the Americans in Vladivostok (speaking for themselves and not as representatives of the State or Navy departments), only a specially selected, limited number of responsible Soviet officials and frequently their wives and/or secretaries were permitted to mix with the Americans. The "mixing" would have to be done because of a particular occasion: most often at a formal party celebrating an historical event or the arrival or departure of a United States official.

Edmund Clubb, a serious-minded, hard-working State Department employee with more interest in and love for the Russians than most foreign service careerists, was our consul-general in Vladivostok during 1944-1945. Clubb, who is now in Mukden, made persistent and strenuous efforts during his stay in the Soviet Far East to become acquainted with the people. He paid formal calls on the secretary of the Party and the governor of the Maritime Province. But he was never received by them. He and his wife both attempted to meet the people—any of the people. Once, out of desperation and boredom, Mrs. Clubb gave a big formal reception and invited all the eligible Russians in town. Nobody came. There was no "occasion"—*i.e.* Red Army Day, Roosevelt's birthday, or the anniversary of the German invasion.

Clubb studied diligently and made excellent progress in learning the Russian language. Despite his friendliest overtures he was constantly rebuffed. Finally he gave up and went off to another assignment, rather embittered.

Thus, as a result of what seems to be a conscious Soviet

policy, the Americans in Vladivostok are isolated. Some think the purpose is to induce the closing of the consulate.* In addition to their servants, the only Russians with whom the Americans have regular contact are the clerks at the small diplomatic food store (operated solely for the American and the Chinese consulates, the only resident foreigners in Vladivostok) and a Soviet naval officer assigned to diplomatic liaison work. This official is cordial and correct in his contacts with the Americans; but he has no key to the closed door that shuts them off from other Vladivostokians.

Little Man from Manchuria

During my second morning in Vladivostok I was awakened by the booming of four- and six-inch coastal guns. In the evening there was anti-aircraft firing. The Americans claimed that a twenty-four-hour alert was maintained by the Vladivostok garrison and that target practice was continual.

"You know," one American told me, "after Churchill's speech things became much tougher for us here. The people really thought there would be war with England within two weeks. They were badly frightened."

I later talked with a black-moustached Russian trade official whom I had met a few months previously in Mukden (Manchuria) and with several Red Fleet men who were playing pool in a smoke-filled room off the lobby of the hotel. In every conversation which touched on world affairs the Russians immediately mentioned two things: the atomic bomb and Churchill's speech in Fulton, Missouri. The bomb

* In August 1946 the United States closed its naval mission in Vladivostok.

made them distrustful and nervous; the speech made them distrustful and angry.

I couldn't get away from the trade official. He hung around the hotel lobby and nabbed me whenever I came in. He seemed to be there at all hours with his tired, creased face and suit.

"There was a lot of grumbling, a lot of grumbling, I don't mind saying," the little trade official told me in English, his moustache twitching like Groucho Marx's. "No consumer goods. Or very little. More tanks instead of streetcars for Vladivostok. They tell me that people began to be openly critical against the Party planners. They expected when Germany and Japan were defeated that things would get much better. Well, I tell you they *are* better, but not *much* better. Then after Churchill's speech was reported the grumbling stopped. Like that!" He snapped his fingers. "And no repressive measures were taken. None were needed. None at all. Churchill's speech did the trick. It taught us that the Party leadership was right. We cannot relax in the face of such warmongers as that." He sighed. "It is very sad, but we cannot have security and new streetcars too." He grinned and patted me on the back. "Only in America you can have both, I suppose, with your atomic bomb."

The little man from Manchuria was anxious to hear about the latest developments in China and especially in Mukden. He was curious about the fate of his friends in the Intourist Hotel in Mukden. I told him that Russians, Red or White, had become extremely unpopular in Manchuria owing to the stripping of the factories by the Red Army.

35

"I know," he said, "that's why I got out."   .

"How did you get here from Mukden?" I asked.

"There are ways," he said. He took out a pipe. I couldn't
think of any of the ways unless he had gone up to Harbin
by rail, and the rail line was supposedly cut. He asked me
some more questions about Manchuria, and then I asked him
why the Americans in Vladivostok were so isolated.

"You Americans make me tired," he said, his expression
suddenly becoming nasty, "some people are always offending
you. Have you ever been a Soviet citizen in China? You think
we are not isolated?"

I said, "Well, perhaps before the Red Army . . ."

"Before nothing," his voice was harsh and his accent grated
on my ears. We were standing in the tiny, unfurnished lobby
of the hotel and everyone that passed paused to gaze at us
both with wonderment. "How do you think American troops
behaved here in Vladivostok from 1918 to 1921? And the
Japanese men? And the Englishmen? Not very well, I can
tell you that. They looted and stole and pushed the Bolsheviks around greatly. Yes, I know the history books have
written this more pretty but it was not pretty then."

"That was more than twenty years ago." I wished then that
I knew more about the intervention period than I had gathered from reading General W. S. Graves' *My Siberian Ad-
venture* and talking with Lieutenant General "Bob" Eichel-
berger, who had been an intelligence officer under Graves.

"Not such long time," said the little man, lighting a curved
stem pipe with a fat, squat bowl that was almost as big as
his face. "You see, it is like last moment for me. My brother

was wounded by Americans for walking too close to your barracks." He pointed—as if showing me the spot.

"I'm sorry," I said. "How did it happen?"

"I do not talk about it. It is forgotten." He bit on his pipe. "He died." He spat on the floor.

I climbed upstairs slowly, feeling depressed. In the Intourist office were several of my acquaintances from the *Smolny*. They had been forced to remain on the ship for an extra day because there was no room in the hotel.

"I am going to Moscow on Monday," I said, still thinking about the little man from Manchuria.

"So are we," they said.

Vera, the blonde Intourist girl, waltzed up to me. "Mr. Lauterbach, do you want a companion in your compartment on the train or not?"

This was an unexpected question. The consulate had assured me that the Russians would insist on my riding alone so that I would not have a chance to "contaminate" one of their citizens.

"Please fix me up with a nice *blondinka*," I suggested. Everyone laughed.

"How much food will you want to take along?" Vera inquired. I hadn't gone into detail yet, but the vice-consul had promised that I could draw on their commissary supplies. I told her to order some bread and vodka for me and I would supply the rest. I still had the case of *10 in 1* rations which I had brought from Shanghai.

Nobody Seems to Care

At ten I climbed up the hill to the American consulate to call for Irene, the naval attaché's secretary, who had promised to spend part of the morning walking around the town with me. The policemen (I don't know why we always call them "secret" police, because they wear uniforms and don't attempt to hide) said good morning and saluted.

Irene and I strolled first to the small diplomatic store on Lenin Street. The shelves were well-stocked with foods, including such rarities as cans of coffee and cocoa. Irene was excited: the store had a supply of fresh cucumbers. She ordered some.

Next we went to the two book shops along the same street. The librarians knew Irene and had promised to save her copies of any new Soviet publications that would possibly interest the Americans. This morning Irene was seeking a particular volume of the Soviet encyclopedia, but it wasn't in stock. I asked for an English-Russian dictionary but there were none. I was offered Russian-Rumanian, Russian-Polish, Russian-Bulgarian and Russian-German instead.

Irene chattered away about her experiences in the Far East. She had worked in Khabarovsk with the United States Navy weather station, and she was brimming over with fact and gossip about that. Her Russian was perfect. She explained that her parents were Russian but she had been born in America. Her citizenship status was still not exactly clear as far as the Soviets were concerned. Irene considered herself an American.

AMERICANS IN SIBERIA

What I saw that morning and on subsequent days made me feel that Vladivostok was probably the most unkempt, disorganized Soviet city I had ever visited. Everything was in a state of dis-repair, including the planked boardwalks on the side streets. In newly liberated cities during the war—Kharkov, Odessa, Stalingrad—people seemed to have had more concern for the appearance of their streets and buildings.

One day, driving out of Vladivostok along the main highway, we crossed a wooden bridge. In the floor of the bridge there was a large hole which was not roped off.

"It's been like that for some time," a Navy man said, "nobody seems to care."

Walking along Lenin Street, which is paved and has street-car tracks, I observed that the side streets running off it were cobble-stoned for about twenty feet and then they disintegrated into muddy cowpaths. On 25th of October Street there were several large workers' apartment houses which had been built during the first Five Year Plan. They had undoubtedly been handsome once. They were still impressive for Vladivostok, but doors and windows were missing, paint was chipped, the lawns overgrown.

The parks in Vladivostok—and most Russian cities pride themselves on these—were more like untended vacant lots than places for "Culture and Rest." Along the shoreline the surface of the bay was so spread over with garbage and debris that the water could not be seen.

The people themselves lacked the galvanic spring in their step which characterizes the citizens of Moscow or Leningrad. Their clothing was not any worse than that worn by average

39

Soviet citizens in the west. On the contrary, Vladivostokians occasionally turned up in surprisingly bright Japanese or Chinese silks or prints which sailors had brought in on cargo ships.

Vladivostok had more beggars on its streets than I had ever seen in the Soviet Union except in Tibilisi, the capital of the Georgian Republic. But that had been in 1935. I asked Irene if she knew the reason for the number of destitute people.

"They say they are political prisoners. Nobody will give them jobs when they get out of prison." That was her explanation, but I didn't accept it completely. One strong point in the Soviet penal system has always been that no stigma should be attached to a citizen once he has served his time.

This was one of the many things which the other Americans had told me about life in Vladivostok that I wanted a chance to check on. I had heard reports of "isolation" and "persecution" before from foreigners in the Soviet Union, and often they were vastly exaggerated.

The Big Shots

At my suggestion, Irene took me to the city Soviet building and we called on the mayor or president of the council. His name was Molokov (milk). He was, his plump secretary said pleasantly, too busy to see me. I explained that I would like to interview him when he was free. The secretary took my name, promising to call me at my hotel or to get in touch with the consulate. She never did.

"Why don't you try to see Comrade Pegov?" Irene asked. "He's the *real* big shot in these parts."

"What's his job now?" I had heard of him as one of the Young Communist leaders who had directed the building of the Far Eastern city of Komsomolsk.

"He is secretary of the Communist Party for the Maritime Province."

"Why don't you come with me?"

"Because we have gotten nowhere with him. Maybe you ought to try barging in on him, American style. If you can't, I'll walk slowly ahead and you catch up."

I agreed. At the entrance of the party headquarters Irene left me. I walked in. A guard with a rifle stopped me.

"I would like to talk with Comrade Pegov," I spoke in Russian, "Is he in?"

"I don't know," said the soldier. "Before you can find out you had better go to the Bureau of *Propusks.*"

"Where is that?"

"Up the side street about a block." He gave me the number and I went out and found the Bureau of *Propusks.* It was located in a dingy little log cabin off a side street. I went in. People were waiting. A sign said "Information" over a slit in the wall. I peered in. An old lady, her head wrapped in a shawl, peered back at me through pince-nez glasses.

"What do you need?" she asked. I explained my business.

"A minute," she muttered and slid the panel closed. I could hear her telephoning to Pegov's secretary.

41

The slit was opened. "Do you have credentials?" she asked.

I produced my passport.

"Not good," she said.

I showed her the Soviet visa.

"Not good," she said.

Finally I dug out a *propusk* in Russian which had been issued to me by the Soviet Foreign Office in 1943. I showed that through the slit, explaining that it was old and not valid any longer.

She glanced at it. "This is all right." She gave it back to me and scribbled on a slip of paper. "Sixth floor," she said.

I returned to the building on the main street and handed the slip to the soldier standing guard. He saluted. "Your credentials, please?"

This time there was no waste motion. I flicked the old Foreign Office card in front of his eyes. He saluted again. I started up the blood-red, thick-carpeted staircase. Between the fifth and sixth floors two more guards were posted, these with bayonets fixed on the ends of their carbines. I went through the identification rigmarole with them.

"The first door on the right," one said.

I walked into a spacious, well-furnished reception room. Presently a very attractively-dressed redhead in her thirties stepped out of an office and introduced herself as Comrade Pegov's secretary. She did not speak English.

I told her that I wanted to ask Comrade Pegov a few questions about Vladivostok, its wartime role, its present status, its plans for the future. She nodded. "Won't you sit down?" she said, "I will try and reach Comrade Pegov. He is not in his office now."

I sat down and she came back in a minute with the morning's paper.

"Do you read Russian?" she asked.

"Slowly," I said.

"Do you want to interview Comrade Pegov yourself in Russian or through an interpreter?"

"With an interpreter," I said, "I want to be certain not to misquote him."

Through the door I could hear her telephoning, trying to find an interpreter. Then she asked for a newspaper. She banged down the telephone and walked briskly through the reception room. Five minutes later she was back, her full, handsome face flushed with triumph.

"Here!" she said, like an Indian warrior presenting a rival's head to his chieftain. It was a month-old copy of the Moscow *Daily News*, which is printed in English.

I thanked her. "Do you read English?"

"Slowly," she said and blushed. She went back to her office and resumed the telephoning. In ten minutes she returned, inviting me to come in.

"Unfortunately," she said, "Comrade Pegov will not be in until late. It is suggested that you might like to write out your questions in advance."

I explained that this was not as good as an interview. "Comrade Pegov's answers to my first questions will suggest other questions," I told her. "May I see him, too?"

"Oh, yes," she said, "but this will speed up things."

"May I write them in English."

"Please."

I spent forty minutes covering three sheets of paper with questions. I wanted to know about the condition of the streets, the bread ration, the isolation of the Americans, demobilization, reconversion, population trends; whether a "concentration camp" I had heard about near the city was really that and if any political prisoners were there, how many Japanese were working in Vladivostok. I asked about the province's leading products, exports, plans for the future. I appended a short biographical note stating that I had interviewed many other Soviet officials and that I was not a "Fascist beast."

The redhead accepted the sheets, inquired how long I would be in town and promised to call me. She never did. The morning of my last day in Vladivostok I called her. She was sorry but Comrade Pegov had left town and would not be back until the following day. We were both sorry. Ten minutes later one of the Americans saw Pegov at his home, near the consulate, getting into his car.

During four busy days in Vladivostok I never reached a Soviet official who would discuss local conditions. I did ask casual questions of a soldier, a waitress, a little boy, and Vera. But their replies were hardly authoritative. None of them except the soldier had ever been out of Vladivostok. To them the city seemed relatively glamorous and modern. As for the concentration camp, the soldier guessed that political prisoners might be there "or elsewhere."

In fairness to the officials that I called on, they were undoubtedly extremely busy, overworked functionaries who had never before received a foreign reporter and would just as soon skip the initiation. If I had stayed for months I might eventually have broken them down.

"Missing" Japs

In Vladivostok I had a fair amount of freedom. I walked or drove where I wanted, photographed what I wanted. I saw loosely-guarded Japanese prisoners clearing rubble and could have spoken to them at length if I had known more Japanese and if they had known more English. As it was, our conversation went something like this:

Jap prisoner, in English: "Cigarette?"

My answer, in Japanese: "Yes." This brought forth a hopeful torrent of Japanese. I said, in Russian, "I don't understand." He was crestfallen.

Jap, in English: "You American?"

My answer, in English: "Yes. How long have you been here?"

His answer, in Russian: "I don't understand."

I repeated my question in Russian. He still didn't understand. I gave him another cigarette and moved on to another prisoner. I finally found one who understood a little more Russian. He said that most of the prisoners had been in Vladivostok for five or six months. They had come from northern Korea. They ate well enough but missed their rice, they had to work too hard, they were anxious to return home.

"Do you like the Russians?" I asked.

"It is difficult to say, your honor," said the Japanese, swiveling his eyes around. "I like Americans better. Have you please cigarette?"

I gave him one, reluctantly.

"Are you given any political education by the Russians?"

"I do not think so," he said, "I am new here."

"I thought you were here five or six months."

"Not me," he said, bowing, "I have been in Khabarovsk. There—no education, only hard working on railroad."

I inspected the city's only department store and was surprised at the variety of goods for sale. Nobody seemed to be buying them. I gathered after asking a few questions that postwar wages in Vladivostok were not high enough to enable the citizens to buy electric toasters at 2,000 rubles.*

"During the war, yes," said a girl clerk. "But now overtime has been dropped in the canneries and in the shipyards."†

Vladivostok had two dramatic theaters and several movie houses. The flossiest, on Lenin Street, was showing the prewar, Hollywood-made musical, *The Great Waltz*, which had been a great favorite in Moscow *circa* 1943. The only other tribute to American culture which I observed on Lenin Street was a dry cleaning establishment which was called *Amerikanka* (The American Woman).

In common with every Soviet city, Vladivostok had its

---

* The official rate of exchange is 5.3 rubles to the dollar. The diplomatic rate is 12 rubles to the dollar.

† On August 25, 1946 the Soviets announced a twenty percent pay increase for workers in the Urals and Siberia.

full quota of watch repair shops and commission stores for the buying and selling of second-hand items. But there appeared to be an unusually large number of hairdressers' salons for women. One of the Vladivostok Americans explained this as "the only symptom of a postwar neurosis which the city's economy could afford."

After lunch that day I continued my inspection of the city. In a borrowed car I drove around the *Zolotoi Rog*. In one of the inner harbor there were a half dozen submarines, quite a few Lend-Lease landing barges, and two new heavy cruisers, the *Kalinin* and the *Kaganovich*. These 8,000-ton ships had been constructed in the great shipyards at Komsomolsk and then transported down the Amur River to the northern Pacific port of Nikolaevsk.

On one of the ridges overlooking the harbor I drove past an unfinished housing development. Thirty or forty one-family cottages had been nailed together with boards ripped from Japanese crates. An attempt was being made at terracing and planting and in a few years—when the shrubs appear and paint is applied to the walls—the development undoubtedly would have a sprucer appearance. The cottages were reserved for Red Fleet officers and their families and several had already moved in, although the houses were as yet incomplete.

In other sections of the city one or two brick buildings were under construction; but work was moving ahead very slowly. I passed them every day for four days but I never saw a fresh brick being added. I would have liked to question Mayor Molokov or Secretary Pegov about this because there is probably an excellent reason or rationalization for the apparent lack of speed in construction work. What it could be, I do not know. If the Russians can organize giant housing projects in the Moscow area, they should be able to do it, at least half as well, in the Far East.

Concentration Camps and Sunday Fun

On Sunday, my third day in Vladivostok, all of us Americans played volleyball behind the house where the vice-consul lived. Later we piled into two cars and went for a drive. First we went to the center of town so I could photograph a white wooden frame church not much bigger than a large hot dog stand. I'd been told it was the only church in the Far East and that it had been opened for Easter services in 1944. According to the other Americans, it was much too small to accommodate all the Russian Orthodox faithful who wanted to worship every Sunday.

I had finished taking the picture when a civilian came up to me and demanded to know whether or not I had permission to use a camera. I yanked out my passport.

"Oh, you're a foreigner," he said, and went away, muttering phrases which sounded uncomplimentary.

On the main road leading out of the city we passed a Red Army encampment. Most of the men were living in tents. A little farther, the big, white brick barracks which had housed American intervention troops in 1918 ("still the best damn buildings in Vladivostok" bragged a navy man) were now being used for a Red Army infantry school. In the field in front of the barracks a soccer game was being played.

Following at a discreet distance behind our station wagon was a nondescript sedan containing the "angels" (security police). When we slowed down, they slowed down. When we stopped, they stopped.

Alongside a barbed-wire enclosed concentration camp, purportedly full of political prisoners, we halted long enough for me to take photographs. From the color of the wooden posts and the new wire, I judged that the camp's outdoor pen had been recently enlarged. This the Navy men affirmed.

"Families and friends of the prisoners come out from town on Sunday and visit with the inmates," one of my companions said.

Less than twenty minutes outside of Vladivostok along the main road we were in real country. The woods had a fresh, clean smell which contrasted sharply with downtown Vladivostok, where the air was heavy with the mingled scents of fish, sea-weed and tar. The area we were now passing was sparsely settled. Here and there would be a simple, wooden country house or *dacha*.

"Every summer they build'em, every winter they tear'em down," Grayson remarked, referring to the *dachas*.

I asked why.

"I dunno. I suppose firewood. But they sure fall to pieces in the winter."

The others in the car agreed.

"That one over there, now," said Grayson, "the one getting a coat of paint. That belongs to Comrade Pegov."

Comrade Pegov's *dacha* was hardly anything spectacular

—just a rambling board bungalow nestled in a clearing and surrounded by tall pines. What set it off from the others was the pinkish paint. If Comrade Pegov was responsible for the inefficient management of Vladivostok, at least he was not deriving a fortune from it.

We parked among the birch trees near the Nineteeth Kilometer. I walked up the railroad tracks a half-mile to the new sanatorium of the Pacific Fleet at Okeanskaya. It was a fancy pink birthday cake building with lots of statues and non-functional froufrou. After the drabness of Vladivostok, the sanatorium was rather a pleasant sight.

Two sailors standing guard at the entrance regarded my camera with suspicion.

"Who are you?" asked a Red Fleet officer. He had a girl in one hand and a Leica camera in the other.

"I'm an American correspondent."

"Good. You can take our picture. Here." He handed me his Leica. I took several shots of him and his girl with the building in the background. He offered to do the same for me, but I told him I was conserving my film.

From the sanatorium we wandered back to the beach. I had to pay a few rubles to get in. Ice cream and candies were being sold everywhere. There was a shooting gallery and a volleyball court, both well patronized. An open-air dance pavilion was crowded, and the orchestra was playing prewar American jazz.

"Look at the Red Fleet men dancing together," Roullard said. "They won't allow them to do that in town at the night club."

AMERICANS IN SIBERIA

There were no fancy private *cabanas,* no public bath-
houses at this beach. Bathers either came in their suits or
changed, with as much modesty as possible, behind upheld
towels or convenient bushes. Of course, many didn't bother
with these amenities and changed quite openly. Nude bathing was no longer allowed. But some of the makeshift garments for swimming would scarcely satisfy Boston's Watch
and Ward Society.

Everyone on the beach was having fun: the young couples
splashing in the water, the children building sand castles,
the sailors on leave hitting bulls-eyes at the rifle range, the
mixed teams pushing around the volleyball court, the relaxed
sunbathers sprawled on the narrow strip of sand, the older
men reading the Sunday paper in the shade, the sweethearts
holding hands on the benches.

"It is funny," Ryan said to me, "They look so unimpressive,
so dismal in the city during the week. Then they come out
here on their free day and have a whale of a time. They have
so little, but they *really* seem to enjoy that little, don't they?"

"They do. It's a better life than they've ever had."

The lifeguards wore full navy uniform and kept watch
from a high wooden tower. A couple of American cigarettes
won me access to their vantage place and I shot a few over-all
pictures of the beach.

Two tall, well-built Soviet bathing beauties were reclining
near the water's edge wearing fascinating two-piece black
silk swim suits. I tried to get them to pose for a picture.
They fled, giggling, into the water.

Walking back to our car we were nearly run down by a

tipsy sailor driving a jeep at high speed through the thickest part of the Sunday crowd. We were all quite mad but the Russians seemed to think it was a pretty funny trick. By some miracle, nobody was hurt.

Siberian Stork Club

In the evening we went to the *Zolotoi Rog*, Vladivostok's only nightclub. It was an old restaurant built at the turn of the century and it had all the atmosphere of a western frontier saloon. The men were men and they didn't know when to stop drinking or when to stop dancing. The sweaty seven-piece band banged out sentimental Soviet ditties, stately tsarist waltzes and prewar American jazz with equal enthusiasm. The Americans, according to custom, were assigned to the best spot—a balcony overlooking the dance floor. This room was already occupied by two of the local citizenry. The anxious manager quietly tried to ease them out, but we protested and invited the Russians to stay and finish their beer. They accepted. They were admiring a copy of *Ogonyok*, the biggest and best Soviet weekly magazine. This was a special anniversary issue marking the first year after the victory and *Ogonyok* had outdone itself in heroic portraiture. Upon learning that I was a correspondent for *Life*, the Russians were anxious to hear my opinion of the issue. I thumbed through it and remarked that it was a very good issue and that the magazine seemed much improved.

This pleased one of the Russians so much that he struggled to his feet, tried to embrace me, and told me that I was indeed "a very attractive and agreeable person."

When the two Russians departed I went downstairs to dance with the secretary of our vice-consul.

After one of the dance numbers, an inebriated artillery captain with uncombed hair and a slept-in uniform staggered over and wrapped his arms around me.

"*Amerikanetz!*" he cried, "*moi droog!*"

I disengaged myself quickly. The captain was hurt by my lack of affection.

"Don't you remember Bucharest?" he said bitterly, "wonderful, beautiful Bucharest?"

I tried to get across the idea that I had never been in Bucharest in my life.

He shook his head sadly. "You correspondents," said he, straightening my uniform, "you are so friendly to us Russians in Bucharest. But here you are afraid."

Another Red Army officer rose from a table and pulled the captain aside. They talked in loud whispers. The inebriate shouted after me as I walked away, "Oh, so you are with American naval officers! You are afraid to remember old Russian friends with them around. Well, it's all the same." The other man led him away and I went upstairs to rejoin my friends. I didn't know if the "it's all the same" meant "never mind" or "it's the same with you as it is with me." I finally decided he had said the former but meant the latter.

Pens and the Press

Next morning I went to the local telegraph office with Lieutenant Commander Ryan. I wanted to discover if I

53

could file a story to New York directly from Vladivostok. A day or so later the telegraph authority replied I could file stories but they "would probably go through Moscow." Having heard rumors of "blind" censorship in Moscow, I decided to wait. In the telegraph office an old woman greeted Ryan as we came in. "She rents pens," said my friend. "Formerly you obtained pens at the window but they disappeared. Then they decided to make you pay a five ruble deposit. But the pens still disappeared. Where else can you get a good pen for five rubles? They raised the deposit fee to ten rubles. Then the customers began to complain about the triple queue. One queue to get a pen, one to send your telegram, another to get your deposit and give the pen back. So they solved it by hiring this old *babushka* to keep track of the pens. She quits promptly at seven every night and she has been known to grab a pen right out of a customer's hand at the stroke of seven."

In the telegraph office I overheard a Red Army lieutenant shouting that a telegram which took only two days to come all the way from Leningrad took two weeks to be delivered to him in Vladivostok although he lived just around the corner from the telegraph office.

"Soviet efficiency," said Ryan. "It's easier for us to telephone Moscow than to reach the diplomatic store a few blocks away."

I had long ago learned in Moscow that when you can't get information any other way in the Soviet Union, the only recourse is to read the newspapers. In the Intourist office at the hotel I leafed through the file of the Vladivostok *Red Banner*.

The city was a large demobilization point for the Red Army and Fleet. The paper was filled with recurring editorial pleas to veterans urging them not to return homeward to the West but to settle in Vladivostok.

The Americans had recently been to see a performance of Maxim Gorki's play, *The Lower Depths*, at the local theater. They had mentioned that the review of the play was worth reading. I found it. The paragraph they had enjoyed stated that since the revolution the horrible conditions depicted by Gorki in *The Lower Depths* no longer existed in the Soviet Union. However, the reviewer went on, the play still pertains to places like the United States of America where there are already five million unemployed.

The foreign news which Tass cabled out to Vladivostok did not help to brighten the picture of life in the English-speaking world. The commentator Matyushkin wrote that "at present reactionary circles in the U.S.A. and Great Britain are in every way cultivating a new variation of the race theory as to the superiority of the Anglo-Saxon race and its 'right' to world domination. They are trying to hand something like an ultimatum to those peoples which do not speak English and threaten them with the inevitability of war if they refuse."

A few days later the foreign news page of the *Red Banner* printed American reactions to President Truman's labor policy. All the quotes were from individuals pro-labor and anti-Truman. Another article told of the effect of strikes on

55

United States production; another reported the prospect of a general strike in Rochester; a fourth, the same day on the same page, predicted a strike of all seamen.

The paper of the next day, June 2, continued quoting attacks on Truman's labor policy. Tass' main source was Johannes Steel, the radio commentator. From Teheran, Tass charged that the British had not yet evacuated their troops from Bushire on the Bahrein Islands. A Moscow foreign news reviewer pointed out that the new Japanese cabinet was not very democratic; and that the General Bor had been warmly welcomed in New York City although he was a Polish reactionary fascist opposed to the present democratic government of Poland, which was duly recognized by Washington as well as by Moscow.

The *Red Banner* for June 3 had three items on its foreign page: the United States Senate had passed Truman's anti-labor bill (the Case Act); a Uruguayan newspaper had lambasted United States policy in Latin America; and a group of British scientists had demanded international control over atomic energy.

While I sat in the Intourist office reading the paper, Vera came in. I asked her what had happened to Johnny, Fritz and Anya.

"They have left," she said.

"How? Where?"

Vera shrugged and didn't answer. Later on the train the other "new" Soviets from the *Smolny* informed me that Johnny, Fritz and Anya had been flown to Moscow.

"What was the urgency?" I teased, "the approach of motherhood or of atomic energy?"

Poppa, with more humor than I had expected from him, replied, "The urgency was motherhood but the priority was atomic."

If I had pressed the matter, I probably could have flown, too. But since I had returned to Russia to make the trip by the Trans-Siberian, I did nothing more than inquire about air transport. There were long, deadly stretches across Siberia when I wished that I had gotten on a plane.

On Monday evening the Americans drove me to the station. I had bought cans of peaches, tomatoes, boned turkey, corn and fruit juices from the consulate commissary. That and my case of *10 in 1*, plus the six huge loaves of white bread and the half dozen bottles of vodka which Vera had procured for me, made my luggage rather heavy. Grason, who had made the Trans-Siberian trip a half dozen times as a courier, suggested that I load up with copies of American magazines, especially *Amerika*, which has Russian text. So all of us were carrying something of mine as we squeezed our way between baggage cars and freight trains to get to the Trans-Siberian Express.

The platform was crowded. A group of Intourist officials were there to pave the way for a Red Army general from Tokyo. With help from the other Americans I managed to stow my stuff in the tiny blue-walled compartment. My roommate, if I was to have one, had not shown up yet.

Shortly before train time he arrived with twenty-four pieces of luggage. It was the man in the brown suit who had eaten with the captain of the *Smolny*.

"I should have asked for a compartment alone," I moaned to Ryan.

"It's not so bad," he said. "I had a squalling child in the next room. At least you don't have that."

He was wrong. The squalling child came aboard a few hours later at Voroshilov.

5,800 MILES ON THE TRANS-SIBERIAN
A. Vladivostok to Irkutsk

BEFORE the Trans-Siberian was completed it took a year to travel the 5,800 miles from Vladivostok to Moscow by carriage, ship and reindeer-drawn sleighs. According to the schedule in effect when I left Vladivostok, "express" trains departed from the east coast port late in the afternoon every Monday, Wednesday and Friday and arrived in Moscow on the morning of the twelfth day. Recently the Vladivostok newspapers have been promising their readers that the pre-war nine-day "super-luxury-express" service would be restored and the entire Trans-Siberian line rehabilitated. The new Five-Year Plan, which I saw advertised on Vladivostok's streets, calls for a 40 per cent increase in freight loadings on railroads of Siberia and the Urals, and 25 per cent of the entire capital for railroad repair and construction is being allotted to these areas.

The shortest and most direct Vladivostok-Moscow rail line, and the first one built (1902), cuts across Manchuria on the

tracks of the Chinese Eastern Railroad. Resumption of this
service will necessarily await the return of peaceful conditions in Manchuria; the Chinese Communists play no
favorites when it comes to severing rail lines.

After the Russo-Japanese War of 1905, Moscow realized
that its Far Eastern provinces could be cut off at any time by
hostilities in Manchuria. In 1908 a second line was begun,
this one all on Russian territory. This route runs northward
to Khabarovsk and then turns westward following the curve
of the Amur River, skirting to the north of the Manchurian
border and south of Lake Baikal. It was completed in 1916
at an estimated cost of a half-billion dollars.

The Soviets, after they had consolidated their hold on
Siberia in 1923, did much to improve the high, narrow road-
beds, the light tracks, obsolete tunnels, and switches on this
route. Work on double-tracking the section from Lake Baikal
to the East was pressed forward. At the same time plans were
drawn and carried out in great secrecy to construct an east-
west trunk line farther north which would be less vulnerable
to Japanese attacks from across the Manchurian border.
Thousands of youthful volunteers and political prisoners
were assigned the tremendous task of pushing a railroad across
the frozen tundra, eventually effecting a junction with the
main route near Nizhneudinsk from Komsomolsk through
Kirensk and north of Lake Baikal. This new line is called
BAM (Baikal-Amur-Magistral), and was extended from Komsomolsk to the Pacific port of Sovietskaya Gaven, north of
Vladivostok.

Passengers on Number 5

My train was called the Number 5. Its pre-World War I locomotive was hooked up to ten wooden cars: a mailcar, restaurant car, an "International" *wagon-lit* type sleeper, three "soft" cars (with bedding) and four "hard" cars (without bedding). One of the "soft" cars was marked "Reserved for women with small children," and one of the "hard" cars was for veterans. The cars had stood out in the broiling sun all day, and the compartments were stifling.

"Shall we open the window?" I asked my roommate. He and his male secretary were busy rearranging their boxes and baggage as the train pulled slowly out of Vladivostok towards its first stop, about ten minutes distant.

The man in the brown suit replied in Russian, "we must choose—either heat or dirt. I suggest we keep our windows closed. When we wish to be cool we can sit in the corridor or walk at a station. But if you wish the window open, I will ask Victor Ivanovich to open it for us."

Victor Ivanovich, the secretary, nodded. I said *"Neechevo"* and went and sat in the corridor. There was no room to sit in the compartment, and at this point I again wished I had insisted on having a "coupé" to myself.

At a big, stone station called Ogolnaya, a half dozen Red Army soldiers tried to force their way onto the International car. The two porters kept them out by force. The senior porter was a bent, bald old man; his assistant was a tall, broad-shouldered ex-soldier who wore four medals and one order for valor on his jersey. I don't know how they found out

61

people's names, but I never heard them refer to any of the passengers on our car except in the formal Russian way: given name plus patronymic (Ivan Alexandrovich).

The Red Army general from Tokyo had been installed in the International car. I judged from his insignia and decorations that he was in the air corps and had served with distinction on the western front in defense of Stalingrad and Moscow. A man in his early forties, he had a handsome face with regular features, curly black hair and good shoulders. When he wore full uniform, his sloping paunch was scarcely noticeable. Shortly after the train left Vladivostok the general retired to his compartment, changed, and reappeared, clad in a pair of sky blue Japanese silk pajamas decorated with a pattern that looked like hurricane clouds. The general was very vain about these pajamas; he wore them continuously, so far as I know, until about a half-hour before we reached Moscow. Then he put on his uniform over them.

The general was truly international. In addition to his Japanese pajamas he carried (or rather his aide carried for him) a United States Air Corps canvas flight bag; he used a Zippo to light the Luckies he puffed through a long-stemmed filter. He was also provided with a bountiful supply of American canned goods and army rations.

The general's roommate was a small, middle-aged man who sported a cocoa-colored camel's-hair lounging jacket and matching trousers during the journey. None of us, with the possible exception of the general, ever discovered exactly what this small man did. Quite by chance I learned that he was a party functionary. But what he did, I don't know and he didn't care to say. Somewhere along the line a gang of hooligans flung stones at the train, smashing two windows in our car on the corridor side. The worried *provodniks* laboriously wrote out a statement explaining that the damage to state property had been caused by "persons unknown" and had not been due to their negligence. Important passengers were invited to sign the statement, and a space was left for their "title." The small man, the general, my roommate, and the colonel of engineers who moved in next door, affixed their signatures in that order.

The general's aide, a cheerful, blond senior lieutenant named Vassily Alexandrovich, was as talkative as his chief was taciturn. On our first night out Vassily presented a flowing Japanese silk kimono, orange and green, to the only unescorted female in the car. She was a tall, buxom, middle-aged lady who acted twenty years younger than she appeared. Because she had two of the physical attributes for the calling, I set her down as an opera singer. I didn't learn until the other side of Novosibirsk that she was a Vladivostok postmistress named Julie Fedorovna.

Being the elite of the car, the general and the party functionary received visitors in their compartment but rarely went visiting themselves. The postmistress was a frequent supper guest and several of the officers dropped around to play cards. The elite were friendly enough to me in the corridor or on the platforms of stations, but they never asked me to drop around for a chat or a glass of the Suntory Japanese whiskey the general poured. Once I casually mentioned to the general that he might care to glance at the magazines I had with me. He declined, saying carefully in English: "No, thank you very much."

When I asked Vassily if his general spoke English, the aide replied: "He can say 'No, thank you very much' and 'I will inform you tomorrow' and 'I am sorry to be so late.'" We both laughed. On another occasion I tried to induce Vassily to tell me what the general thought of the United States occupation of Japan.

"Very good, very good," Vassily said, "oh, so very American. Great bargain sale. Two for the price of one."

"How so?"

Vassily began laughing. "Formerly one supreme ruler, now two—" His frame shook with laughter. "Hirohito *and* MacArthur."

"I heard the same joke from Americans in Tokyo."

When Vassily stopped roaring he slapped my shoulder and said, "Of course, I heard it from an American also."

Simple arithmetic indicated that there were more people living in the International car than there were berths. The *provodnik* said two people often bought two first-class tickets and only one berth. They slept in shifts. No sex differentiation was observed in assigning compartments.

The International car's roster (I was the only foreigner) included three well-groomed, quiet-spoken Soviet consular officials; two youthful Red Fleet officers; a bright-eyed Stakhanovite worker from the Vladivostok shipyards traveling with his wife and child to the Caucasus on their first vacation in five years; an inspector of mines representing the Ministry of Non-ferrous Metals in Moscow; and a family of four who lived down at the far end of the corridor and rarely mixed with the rest of us. Occasionally, more passengers boarded the train, but I don't think anybody left before Moscow.

In November 1943 I had journeyed from Baku to Moscow, six days by train at that time. At that period my fellow passengers were all eager to meet an American, to share views, to thank the United States for our canned pork meat and our trucks, to ask when the "second front" would be opened. Now there was definitely more of a barrier. The general and the party functionary set the tune. They were polite, but reserved. Fortunately, not everybody followed their tune.

I made no attempt to "interview" anybody unless they appeared receptive to conversation. Time was on my side. After three or four days, I hoped that boredom would overcome caution. Of course, there were exceptions—frank, friendly people who wanted to understand an American's viewpoint, wanted to express their own.

One of the Red Fleet officers and the inspector of mines had a good working knowledge of English. But it was several days before either of them entered into any kind of conversation with me. Toward the latter part of the trip they became more cordial and helped me out when I was unable to translate a Russian expression even with the dictionary.

Very Good Eisenhower

That first evening long, serpentine columns of oil tank trains passed us heading toward Khabarovsk and away from Khabarovsk. The majority of cars were formerly German with the Nazi railroad insignia almost obliterated.

Three hours north of Vladivostok the train halted for more than half an hour at the town of Voroshilov. There was a quick exodus from our train and a race for the *kipyatok* (hot boiled water) spigot. Passengers waited in line holding pails, buckets, canteens, thermos bottles, kettles, samovars—anything that would hold liquid for evening *chai* (tea). This water-rush was repeated at every good-sized station.

After a sharp, high warning bleat, the locomotive lurched forward. At that moment and only then the passengers scrambled for the train. The cars creaked, squeaked, groaned forward. Once, out of boredom, I experimented and discovered that I could comfortably dally until the train really got moving and then still catch it easily before the last car cleared the station platform; this and balancing on one rail like a tight-rope walker plus pacing platforms was all the exercise I managed for twelve days.

It was at Voroshilov that the railroad engineer with the rank of colonel boarded the train and moved into the compartment adjoining ours. He was accompanied by a very pregnant wife and two very sleepy children. A half dozen of the colonel's extrovert friends pushed onto the car to wish them farewell and to gulp another last swig of vodka. They didn't leave until the train broke its inertia with a series of shudders. Then the men, with great gusto, all bussed each other smack on the lips. The women just shook hands.

The sky was so light we didn't need electricity until after ten. And then the lights didn't work; something was wrong with the fuse box. When it was repaired I spread out copies of *Amerika*, the United States Information Service picture magazine published in Russian. My roommate and his secretary, who were still rearranging their gear to permit sitting room in the compartment, were hot and tired. I showed them the magazines. The roommate was uninterested. He preferred a paper-bound translation of Balzac's *A Woman of Thirty Years*. But his blond, muscular secretary liked pictures. First he gasped over New England scenery in color and then he was even more fascinated by the flattering portraits of America's military leaders. He pointed to Eisenhower.

"Very wonderful general," he said in Russian. Then he tried in English, "General . . . very good, yes?"

I agreed.

"So is Zhukov," he said, relapsing into Russian. I agreed again. Victor Ivanovich grinned, revealing two even rows of strong white teeth. He put out his hand and grabbed mine. We were friends.

By 1 A.M. the coupe was in shape so that the old *provodnik* could come in, pull down the berths, and make them up with bed linen. My berth was the lower, and it was very comfortable—the first night. Since it was left down all the way to Moscow it soon acquired a crinkly sprinkling of bread crumbs and other food sundries, which were not satisfactorily covered by the thickening veneer of soot that gathered from day to day—with windows closed.

Victory for Russia

The first morning I awoke early but resolved to remain in my berth until my roommate roused himself. He slept soundly and relatively silent in spite of the incessant yammering of the colonel's infant in the next compartment. Unable to doze, I killed time by counting the hours which the trip would require before we finally reached Moscow. The total came to an awful figure like two hundred and seventy-eight. Then I broke it down. If I slept ten hours, spent two hours eating, one hour walking around stations and three hours reading, I would still have to find diversions for the other eight hours every day. By the end of the first week I had revised my figures: I slept more, walked more, read more, talked more and spent a longer time eating.

About eleven my roommate rolled out of bed. He felt his face. He had a tough beard. "Shall we shave today or tomorrow or not until Moscow?" he asked.

"Not until Moscow."

He laughed and went into the washroom. "You will change your mind," he said. "Tomorrow we will shave because it will be a big event, a job to do, yes?" He was right.

At breakfast I could see he was going to be difficult. Victor Ivanovich brought us hot water in a Japanese thermos.

"Tea?" my roommate suggested.

"Coffee," I said. "I have some. You have tea, I'll have coffee."

"No coffee," he said. "I have tea."

"Oh, don't you like coffee?"

"*Neechevo.* I have tea," he repeated.

"I have coffee."

We sat there, the hot water cooling in our faces.

"What about cocoa?" I asked. His face brightened.

"Fine," he said, "I have cocoa up there." He pointed to

the top of the stack of boxes piled precariously on a shelf. He started to mount the ladder.

"Mine is right here." I had put my food box under the table.

He pretended he didn't hear and brought his down. So we drank his cocoa.

I let him get away with it. The American press would have billed it, "VICTORY FOR RUSSIA AT BREAKFAST." Thereupon I decided on a "tough" policy. The next morning I *insisted* on coffee. The Russian acepted his "defeat" without a word. On subsequent mornings we drank both coffee *and* cocoa. Tea was relegated, by mutual agreement, to supper.

Our breakfast was large and varied: fruit juice, salami, sardines, cheese, peanut butter, jam, and lots of bread. My roommate sliced the bread: twelve pieces. He ate six, scolded me for consuming only two-and-a-half. The leftover bread and fish we gave to the porters.

We went through the Alphonse-Gaston act with cigarettes. He was smoking Camels and he had a dozen or more cartons with him. I was smoking another brand, not by choice. He gave me a carton of Camels when he found out I liked them; I presented a carton of mine to Victor Ivanovich.

On that first morning, while we were smoking, my roommate handed me his card. His name was Michael F. Ageev (Ah-gay-eff) and his title was Deputy Trade Representative of the U.S.S.R. in China. I showed him my card.

"I know about you," he said. "The captain of the *Smolny* told me. Also, I saw you one night dancing at the Mandarin

Club in Shanghai with Mrs. Ravenholt. I knew her and her husband in Kunming."

I said I liked them very much. "I like them, too. They are honest correspondents," Ageev said. "Tell me, where did you learn Russian so very well?"

I protested that I didn't know Russian very well. I had picked up the tourist words—ordering, asking, complaining, buying, drinking—on my first visit to Russia in 1935; I had studied at night school for four months in 1943 before returning to Moscow as *Time-Life* correspondent; I had learned more during a year in the Soviet Union; then recently I had had a little practice in Japan and China; but still I didn't speak "very well."

"But you understand me?" Ageev asked. I did, but said it was easier if he spoke slowly and used simple words. In case of necessity I had a dictionary with me that I'd borrowed from our consulate in Vladivostok.

Ageev wanted to know if I was "friendly" to his country. I assured him that I was. He said he liked America and he began to talk about it. In the course of his remarks I learned that, in common with most Russians I have met, he also admired Deanna Durbin, the American air force, Camel cigarettes, United States canned goods and gin. Then he inquired if I'd seen a certain movie. The name didn't sound familiar in Russian. It turned out to be *Winged Victory*. I hadn't seen it.

"That movie," said Ageev, "was playing in twenty-seven theaters in San Francisco at one time. Is that right?"

I didn't know. And I didn't know how he knew. Before I could ask him, he was off on labor in America.

"Is the great coal strike settled?" he inquired.

I shook my head. I didn't know that, either. "I only know what I read in the Vladivostok *Red Banner*," I said. Ageev did not smile. "Speaking of Vladivostok," I hurried on, "I thought conditions there were very bad."

"I was born there," said Ageev irrelevantly. He smoked in silence. "The city became very bad during the war."

"But I have been in many Soviet cities—cities that were actually at the front. They were better than Vladivostok."

"That is true," he said wearily and slowly, "war is the excuse, certainly. But I do not know how long that will be a good reason for a bad city like Vladivostok. It is really quite bad."

He thought in silence for a minute and then said, "Look here, it is impossible to say Vladivostok was not at the front. It deteriorated for the same reasons as other cities—without German shelling or occupation. No trained people to do the job. The winter is cold but there is no heat because the coal is used on the railroad. That ruins apartments. Pipes burst. You cannot so quickly forget the war, my dear."

I told him I had been willing to find out the reasons for the apparent inefficiency in the city but that neither the mayor nor the Party secretary would see me.

"That is bad," said Ageev. "You must understand that this is very far from Moscow, which is our center. It takes a long time for things to reach Vladivostok. Not only consumer goods but orders and laws and actions of the spirit.

It is an outpost of our country still. Perhaps not all our best people are there. They are more needed elsewhere."

I was silent.

"Cities are strange," said Ageev, philosophically. "Have you ever been to New Delhi or Calcutta? Or to Bagdad? Indian cities I do not like. In a British hotel in Calcutta where I stayed I was all the time confused by small boys coming in and out of my room. One to carry my bags, one to draw the shades, one to fix the mosquito netting, one to run a bath, one to brush the shoes. Then if you want to drink or eat, there is one to take the order and one to bring it. It makes you dizzy. And if you are a Russian, it makes you somewhat annoyed, too. Of course they always want *baksheesh*."

This description of life in Calcutta was meant as a subtle reminder to me that all was not well in the capitalist world, either. "I saw many beggars in Vladivostok," I said. "Usually there are not any in Soviet cities—or very few."

"Some political prisoners," said Ageev, matter-of-factly.

"I saw a concentration camp at Second River which is supposedly for political prisoners. Is it?"

Ageev said with a shrug, "Maybe so."

"Why must former political prisoners become beggars?"

"Perhaps they will not take jobs? Perhaps some people will not give them work. I do not know." Ageev picked up his copy of Balzac.

Khabarovsk on the Amur

Early in the afternoon we reached the first big station, Khabarovsk, four hundred and ten miles almost due north of Vladivostok and in the same latitude as Seattle, Washington. Founded in 1858 as a military outpost along the banks of the broad Amur River, Khabarovsk has become one of the most important industrial and trading centers in the Far East. Its rapid growth in the past few decades has been amazing. In 1923, when the Soviets took over the town, there were only thirty-four thousand inhabitants. Today Khabarovsk is a busy city of over three hundred thousand, specializing in the production of building materials, machine tools and electric power. It is the junction point for a spur line which runs up to Komsomolsk, the new city built in the past two decades by Young Communists, most of them under thirty. Crude oil from Sakhalin Island comes to Khabarovsk's cracking plants, where it is refined into aviation gas. Part of the Amur River and the Kamchatka fish catch is canned in Khabarovsk factories.

Perhaps the amount of money, energy and planning expended on Khabarovsk partially accounted for the Soviets seeming disinterest in the deterioration of Vladivostok. The finest new airport in the Far East is not in Vladivostok, but in Khabarovsk. In the last prewar budget approved by the Supreme Soviet, Khabarovsk was allotted the heaviest capital expenditures for any area of the U.S.S.R. Today it is the largest tin and the second largest gold producing center in the Soviet Union.

Near this sprawling, unfinished city with its wide dirt roads and big, roughly-finished brick apartment houses and plants, the United States Navy opened a weather observation post. This was done in the winter of 1945 as the result of an agreement reached at Potsdam. The weather station provided storm warnings for Allied sea and aircraft operating in the Pacific area during the war against Japan. When the war ended abruptly, the Americans requested and received grudging permission for the meteorologists to remain. But on December 20, 1945, the Rusians, without explanation, requested that the Khabarovsk station and a similar one at Petropavlovsk on Kamchatka, be discontinued.

The Navy men who worked in Khabarovsk were not happy. The climate was cold and the attitude of the Soviet officials even colder. The weather stations were surrounded by barbed wire and Russian guards and no American, not even the commanding officer, could leave the premises without permission. Navy personnel were allowed "liberty" in the city only two days a week. They complained that they were permanently "under observation" even then. Added to these restrictions were worse than usual headaches over red tape involved in arranging for necessities: food, transportation and heat.

"But," one of the men who had been there told me, "Khabarovsk is a much livelier town than Vladivostok."

At the Khabarovsk station I wandered around, openly taking pictures. Outside the guarded gates leading to the train platform dozens of people were huddled together on the ground. I talked with them briefly. Several of the families were refugees who had been evacuated from Byelorussia and the Ukraine during the war. Now they wanted to go home and were waiting for trains. Others were new arrivals who had not yet found a place to live in Khabarovsk. They acted sullen and unhappy. During the war I had conversed with people living in the same manner at the Novosibirsk station, and they had understood why they must wait without adequate lodging. These people were resentful.

I joined the queue at a kiosk to buy a local newspaper. As I started to peruse it, a policeman approached me and saluted.

"You have been taking pictures," he stated. I nodded. "Please close your camera and come with me." I followed him into a small office in the station. Pictures of Stalin, Kaganovich and Voroshilov adorned the bare walls. The policeman asked me to sit down. I lit a cigarette, gave him one.

"May I see your papers, please?" He took my passport, looked at the picture and then at me. "So you are an American correspondent?"

"I am an American correspondent."

"Do you not know that this is a military zone and it is forbidden to take pictures in a station without permission?" He was quite nice about it.

"I thought the war was over."

"You have no permission. How much film have you taken?"

"Quite a lot. But I have been taking pictures in Vladivostok, too."

"What interests you so much here?"

"The station, the people, the kiosk. Everything I see."

The blue-uniformed policeman asked when I had entered his country and where. I told him and added, "That camera and the films were with me at the customs in Vladivostok.

I was permitted to enter with the camera and the film. I am a correspondent. I work for a picture magazine. Why would I be allowed to come to your country with film and a camera if I am not allowed to take pictures?" I opened the passport and pointed to the page where the green-hatted captain had inscribed the number of my Rolleiflex.

The policeman stood up, closed my passport and handed it back to me. "You will not take any more pictures in Khabarovsk, please." He saluted.

"I have enough. Thank you."

On the platform I met Poppa, the figure skater. I told him what had happened.

"A bureaucrat," he scoffed. "Russia has always been full of them. But they let you keep the camera? Good."

The most prominent story on the foreign news page of the June 11th Khabarovsk daily paper was a Tass dispatch from New York dated June 7. It read:

"At the town of Columbia in Tennessee, a group of Negroes is being tried for 'attempted murder' by a court whose jury is formed entirely of whites. . . . A 'Committee of Justice in the State of Tennessee' under the Chairmanship of Eleanor Roosevelt has been formed. . . . Although most newspapers are ignoring the trial, the *Daily Worker* and the Negro press give full reports. . . ."*

As I watched other passengers reading their papers I felt sure I would hear about this story before I reached Moscow. I didn't have long to wait.

Just east of Khabarovsk I had caught my first sight of

* In October 1946 the white jury acquitted twenty-three of the twenty-five Negroes.

thousands of Japanese prisoners of war working in their green-gray fatigue uniforms. I pointed them out to one of our *provodniks*—the tall, broad-shouldered younger one. "Why not?" he asked. "If they had won, Russians would have to work for them. They are not badly treated, I believe." After we had left Khabarovsk I sat by a window watching the cattle grazing along the railroad tracks. As the train clanked across a steel bridge over the log-filled Amur River, the young porter came up to me holding in his big, hairy hands a copy of the Khabarovsk newspaper. He pointed to the dispatch from Tennessee. "I think perhaps the Japanese war prisoners here are better treated than the Negroes in the South in America. Is that not so?"

I explained as well as I could that the situations were not analogous. I went into my compartment and found a copy of *Amerika* which had a picture story on Marian Anderson. "There is another side to it," I said. "We are guilty of much injustice to Negroes in America. But many Americans are against such discrimination. Even with the unfairness it is possible for some talented artists such as Marian Anderson to be recognized." He looked at the magazine, I thought, a little suspiciously. He looked at the contents page.

"American propaganda?" I asked, trying to read his unspoken thoughts.

He was hurt. "No. Why do you say it's propaganda? This is quite an *official* magazine. Therefore, it is the truth. Now if this were the Hearst press. . . ." He grinned and accepted a cigarette.

THROUGH RUSSIA'S BACK DOOR

Birobidzhan, the Jewish Region

Later that same day we reached Birobidzhan. The Soviet-operated radio station in Shanghai had recently been broadcasting deliriously delightful descriptions of life in the Jewish Autonomous Region. The area, they said, was replete with "ripe fields of wheat, rye, oats, barley, soya, corn, rice . . . forests burgeoning with cedars, larch, silver firs, oaks, cork, birches . . . mines and quarries laden with gold, tin, manganese, molybdenum, iron, coal, graphite, limestone, marble. . . ." It was impossible to do much checking from the platform. The railroad station was neater and more modern than most of those we had passed. I watched a Jewish family saying farewells to a young girl wearing a Red Army uniform. Her olive drab military blouse had no epaulets, so I judged the girl had recently been demobilized. She climbed onto the coupling between our car and the restaurant, arranged her boxes as a seat and made herself as comfortable as possible.

"Where are you going?" I asked.

"To Krasnoyarsk, to school," she replied. Her name was Olga Borisevna Belikovsky. She wore her dark hair in braids and her plain face had no trace of make-up. During the war she had been a recruiting officer in the Jewish Autonomous Region. "Of a population of one hundred and eight thousand almost forty thousand went to fight the invaders," she said. This seemed an incredibly high figure to me, but later I had a chance to check its accuracy in Moscow. The reason for this unusual percentage was that men of draft age prevailed among the Jewish emigrants.

78

I pressed Olga to tell me whether the life was "good" in Birobidzhan. She was surprisingly candid. "For those who like farming and can do it well, life is very fine. Even during the war there were enough potatoes. But among us Jews who like to trade . . . ?"

"Is it true the region needs specialists and professional people?" The Soviet government had advertised this on the Shanghai radio.

"Yes, all of Siberia does. Perhaps all of Russia. But we very much need doctors and teachers."

"What are you going to study in Krasnoyarsk?"

"I am going to become an animal doctor, a veterinarian."

"Who will pay for your education?"

She was surprised that I could be so ignorant of a fundamental fact. "All demobilized can go to school and the tuition is paid and we receive a salary and clothing and food in addition."

"How much will your salary be?"

"About 200 rubles per month. More if my grades are better than average."

"Ah, capitalist incentive system!"

She laughed. "How can you compare it?" she said. "Everyone receives more than enough to live. The better students, like the better workers in any organization, have the right to receive more."

"What will the new Five Year Plan do for Birobidzhan?"

"We will have a new shoe factory, a new knitting factory, much more electric power. We would have had them now except for the war. It is planned, I read about it, that the region will become the textile center for the Far East. You know during the war the women and children made clothes for the men at the front. Over a half-million pieces."

Argument on Korea

The train had started to move again. Ageev came to see where I was. He suggested that we go into the restaurant car and try a meal. The diner was full of flies and the tablecloths were already soiled. A few Red Army officers were the only customers. We were given a leather-encased bill of fare. We ordered black caviar, black bread, butter, beefsteak with fried potatoes, and coffee. And, naturally, some vodka to go with the caviar. While we exchanged quick toasts and slow conversation in Russian, two air force majors at the next table began debating loudly whether I was English or American. Finally they came over and asked me. I invited them to sit down.

"Where are you coming from?" the blond, fat one wanted to know.

"China."

"We are from Korea. Have you been there?"

I said I had. Then they told me how much they liked American flyers and American airplanes, how they disapproved of American policy in Korea, and how they were happy to be going back to civilian life. The very blond major appeared completely round—his head, his cheeks, his nose and his eyes all seemed symmetrically round. But he was not soft looking. He said his name was Glubov and introduced his long-nosed friend as Frezhenko.

2

"What don't you like about our policy in Korea?" I asked
Glubov. He ordered some more vodka before replying. "You
have thrown out of office all the representatives of the people
who took over from the Japanese. You have brought in exile
leaders from Washington and Chungking that the Korean
people do not want." He referred, of course, to Dr. Syngman
Rhee and Kim Koo.

"How about the Soviet zone?" I countered. "Have all
parties been given political freedom?"

"Certainly," said Frezhenko. He wore three medals on his
chest.

"All those who fought the Japanese and the Korean reactionaries. There is no freedom for those who collaborated,"
added Glubov.

He proposed a toast to "the memory of President Roosevelt" and we drank it, bottoms up. The majors paid absolutely
no attention to Ageev except to clink his glass when a toast
was drunk.

I reminded them that the Communist party existed in our
zone in Korea.

"Would a pro-American party be allowed to operate in
your zone?" I asked. "A party which openly favored capitalist
democracy instead of the Soviet type of democracy."

"Certainly," Frezhenko hiccuped.

Glubov was puzzled. "Korea *is* a capitalist country. But
the peasants want land reform. They must have the land or
they will starve. Only the collaborators and the rich landlords
are in favor of keeping the land away from the peasants.
Naturally there is no freedom for them."

"The great trouble with Korea," I said, coming back to the inevitable platitude about Korea, "is that there is no central administration."

"Exactly," said Frezhenko.

"I agree," said Glubov. He suddenly looked at Ageev, sitting there so quietly in his non-Russian, brown business suit bought on Nanking Road in Shanghai. "What country are you from, comrade?"

"I am a Russian," said Ageev, amused. "Let's have some more vodka. How about you, my dear?" He was addressing me. I nodded.

"About Korea," I began again, "General Hodge told me it's the Soviets who are holding up a joint administration."

"No, it's the Americans," shouted Frezhenko.

"Yes," said the roundish Glubov sagely, "we are willing to have a government of the people, but you want Korea under exiles." I couldn't help recalling a similar argument with a Russian about Poland in 1944. Korea, to the Soviet way of thinking, was the Poland of the Far East.

The argument went on and we kept ordering more vodka. We came to no agreement on Korea. When Glubov began questioning me about the demobilization law in America I found my Russian vocabulary too limited and my tongue slowed up by vodka.

I stumbled badly for Russian words and kept slipping back into English. Glubov's questions were growing more and more technical, and I had more and more difficulty understanding his exact meaning. Without a word of warning, Ageev began translating Glubov's questions for me in very good English. He did it so naturally and easily that I did a very slow double-take. In fact, it was almost an hour later before I realized that he was speaking English for the first time in my presence. His English vocabulary was so much more varied than my Russian vocabulary that I felt a trifle silly. Later on, when I complimented him on his English and chided him for not speaking it sooner, he was embarrassed. "Your Russian is fine. I like to listen to you," he said. "I speak English so badly, my accent. . . ."

Soviet Demobilization

The Soviet law on demobilization, as Glubov described it, contained many of the same kind of benefits as the American G.I. Bill of Rights. There were a few outstanding differences. The G.I. in the Red Army (who was not as well paid as the American G.I.) received a whopping mustering-out bonus equivalent to a full year's pay for each year in the service. Officers, however, received much less: two month's pay for one year of service, three months' for two years, four months' for three, and five months' pay for four years of service.

Every demobilized soldier and officer was entitled to receive his job back in not less than a month's time after leaving the army. Time spent in the Red Army or as a partisan must be counted as time spent in continuous work in the same place. All demobilized men must be permitted to resume their former living quarters, which in roof-poor Russia is an extremely important consideration.

Glubov did not know how many men had been demobilized from the Red Army. "But all men from the oldest draft age, which was fifty-five, down to twenty-seven have been allowed to go home."

"And all women," Frezhenko said.

"In addition," said Glubov, "high school and college graduates, men who were seniors in college, and every enlisted man who suffered a wound at any time during the Great Patriotic War. The total number is many, many millions, as you can see."

I was surprised that Glubov, as indicated by his questions, had some ideas about the American demobilization laws. He was especially sharp in demanding to know the exact stipulation on job and union security. I thought perhaps the Soviet newspapers had been reporting on our demobilization plans, and I inquired where he had picked up his information.

"*Britanski Soyuznik* (British Ally)," he replied, referring to the weekly Russian language newspaper published by the British in Moscow. "It's a very fine journal."

The bill for our lunch—or dinner at that price—came to $60. Caviar, at seven dollars per portion, was the most expensive item. When we had finished our coffee, the major insisted on ordering cognac all around.

Frezhenko, a Ukrainian, told me that he had first met American flyers at Poltava where the United States had an ill-fated B-17 base during the last year of the war. Both majors flew Soviet bombers which they thought were very good ships but not as powerful as the Flying Fortresses.

Glubov broke in on the conversation about airplanes. He gripped my arm hard and his round blue eyes bored straight into mine.

"What was the reaction in America to Churchill's speech at Fulton, Missouri?" he demanded. He pronounced it "Mee-ssour-ee," as if he thought it were three words.

I explained that I had been in the Orient at the time, but that I imagined the public reaction had been somewhat mixed and that opinion had been divided along political lines.

"When I read of that speech," said Glubov, his eyes still holding mine, "I thought there would be war. I don't want war. I want to go home." He fumbled with the buttons on his tunic and drew out a picture. "This is my family. My boy is ten years old; my girl is seven. See! Her legs are very thin. She was in occupied territory. They took my wife in a labor corps. She is dead, without doubt."

Frezhenko said quickly, "I am glad all Americans did not approve Churchill's speech." He fingered his nose thoughtfully. "But maybe it was a good thing, that speech. It made us realize where we stand with certain elements." There was a silence. Frezhenko continued, "Have you been to Manchuria?" I nodded. "Is it true," he asked, slurring his words, "that many American troops are going into Manchuria?"

Glubov put his snapshot away. "I do not believe it," he said.

There were no American troops as such in Manchuria, I said, but American ships and United States planes had helped to transport the Chinese National Army into Manchuria. I expected an argument and quickly put in, "We recognize the Central Government of Chiang Kai-shek, and so does Moscow."

But they were not angry, just relieved that the rumor about

American forces fighting in Manchuria had been exaggerated.
I tried to find out where they had heard it. If it were in
their Red Army political education course or in their army
newspaper, they would not say. All they would say was "in
Korea."

"What have we finally decided about Korea?" Glubov
unexpectedly asked, like the chairman of a meeting anxious
to wipe his agenda clean.

Ageev, who had taken no part in the conversation except
to translate occasionally, said, "Korea should have its independence." I quickly assented. So did Frezhenko. As we
shook hands and said goodbye, Glubov said, "Korea must
be independent in a year or two. Yes, that is so. But the
people must be freed from economic slavery, from landlordism." We promised to meet again.

The train was stopping at Bira, another large town in the
Jewish Autonomous Region. I got off. Olga Belikovsky
jumped down to stretch her stocky cotton-clad legs. As we
paced up and down the platform she asked me about the
life of Jews in America. I replied in generalities, not knowing
where to start. The thing which I said that seemed to impress
her most was that education was free in America and that
nobody was barred because of race, color or creed. Inevitably
she, and most Russians, came back, as a tennis player pounds
an opponent's weak backhand, to the status of the Negroes
in the South. "Can *they* go to *any* schools freely?" she asked.
I had to admit they could not. Then I saw disbelief in her
eyes—she doubted everything I had said about the Jews. I
made up my mind then and there to begin all such future

conversations by quickly and freely admitting and attacking anti-Negro discrimination in America.

Chiang, Blücher, Gorki

The third day was especially long, monotonous and depressing. The sun did not shine. The train plodded along at twenty miles an hour, halting at small villages every few hours. The Russians in my car were visiting each other's compartments, getting up games of *Préference*, dominoes and chess. I cannot play *Préference*, a nonstop, four-handed card game; I am a rank novice at chess; and the Russian version of dominoes is considerably more complicated than the one I played as a child.

There was a run on my stock of magazines. Poppa approached me at a station and asked for reading material, and I gave him a handful of magazines to bring back to his "soft" car. I was launched on a rereading of Tolstoi's *War and Peace*, this time pledged not to skip or skim any of the interminable battle scenes or philosophical tracts.

In the afternoon Victor Ivanovich ordered our midday meal from the restaurant car. There was a daily choice of "*bifshteK*" or "*rrumpshtek*." The former was fried with eggs on top, the latter with onions. Ageev opened a case of his "London Brand" Argentine gin and urged me to drink. I had too much of the bathtub variety as a college undergraduate and have had no taste for it since. Despite all of Ageev's pleading, verbal cudgeling and even sarcasm, I turned him down and drank his health in vodka.

"Vodka!" he scoffed. "It has no taste."

As is the Russian custom, Ageev never drank without eating. He would sit down with his gin bottle, slice a *kolbassa* roll, pour himself half a tumbler of the gin. Then he would pick a slice of *kolbassa*, sniff it, inhale its fragrance, gulp down the gin and then quickly pop the sausage into his mouth. He never appeared to really enjoy drinking but he was always willing to do it.

After dinner I walked down the corridor to the vestibule where the old *provodnik* was chopping wood into little sticks to heat his samovar. He saluted me. "It's nice to see Americans on this car," he said slowly and softly. "It's been a long time. I want you to know this is a very famous car. I am fifty-nine years and four months old. I have been working here for thirty years. The stories I can tell you about the people who have ridden in these compartments! In 1922 or 1923, I forget which year, a Chinese officer . . . do you know who he is now? Chiang Kai-shek. He had berth number 9 in there. I remember him well; he never slept. Then Shvernik, he has been on this train. He is now the chief of the Supreme Soviet in Moscow. And Kalinin, the one who died; he was as old as I am nearly when he was on this train. How the peasants cheered him at the stations! There was one time when this car was part of Vassily Konstantinovich's special train. . . ."

"Who was that?"

"Marshal Vassily Konstantinovich Blücher, an old railroad man himself. He was the biggest and greatest man here in the Far East for many years. He called himself Commander in Chief and President of the Far Eastern Republic."

"What was he like, Marshal Blücher?" I gave the old man a package of cigarettes. He thanked me profusely and blessed my family.

"He was a wonderful man. What a sense of humor! How he could swear!"

I had to fetch my dictionary to get the translation of the word "swear." The old man went right on as if there had not been any interruption. "Blücher was broad and squat with such a little moustache here." He put his fingers under his nose. "He defended Khabarovsk against the White Guards." The old man shook his head. "That Blücher!"

"Where is he now?"

The old porter shrugged his shoulders. "He was very neat for all his roughness. A military man from his boots. But Maxim Maximovich. That's our Gorki. You have heard of him surely? Always with the same baggy trousers, the blue shirt, the sweater high around the neck. He had a big, long moustache and sometimes he did not shave for days. Once before he had to speak to a meeting I shaved him. Right here in front of this samovar I shaved Maxim Maximovich."

I asked Ageev what had happened to Marshal Blücher. "Is he in prison out here somewhere? I remember there was a great mystery about his disappearance."

"No mystery," Ageev said in English. "He went with Tukhachevsky and that gang."

"Was he shot?"

Ageev shrugged. "I do not know, my dear. But I do not think he is now alive."

At nightfall the train arrived at Skorovorodino, a small

station where the engine was watered. Ageev, who had crossed on the Trans-Siberian a half dozen times, turned out to be an encyclopedia of odd facts.

"This place, my dear," he said in English, "is coldest place in all Soviet Union. It is so cold that in winter people here drink 90 per cent alcohol to stay warm and stay from sleep. Vodka makes them sleepy." He went on to say that the subsoil was permanently frozen. "In northern Siberia and here, also, several meters under feet is ice which has not thawed since age of glaciers. Our Soviet scientists come here and dig and find strange specimens of former men. They even say that some forms of animal life which were frozen in ground for hundreds years become alive again. It is really very cold in this place."

I took him at his word, drank some vodka, made five or six pages of notes, put my trench coat over the blanket on my berth and went to sleep.

Siberian Village

At Ksenevskaya next morning the sun was shining brightly. I began taking pictures around the station. Two sailors from the Soviet Pacific fleet came up and asked me to take their pictures. "We have been together four years. Soon we will go our separate ways. We have no picture together." I assured them of my willingness to photograph them, but I had difficulty making them understand that I could not have prints ready before Moscow. A crowd of passengers and townsfolk had gathered around us attracted partly by my uniform, my obviously foreign accent and my camera. As soon as the sailors moved off an eager, red-faced tank officer launched into a long story about how his tank outfit and the Americans linked up in Austria and caught the Germans in a *kessel*. He went so fast I had a difficult time keeping up with him. He noticed it and said, "Do you speak German?" I said I didn't.

"How do you like our country?"

"Very beautiful," I said.

"And the standard of living?"

"*Neechevo*," I said shrugging. I was collecting my Russian for a further definition when he went on. "It's little, I know. I have seen elsewhere. But in five years . . ." he laughed and counted on his fingers in German, "*ein, zwie, drei, fir, funf* . . . it will be better."

"Stalin said so," I said.

"We say so, too," announced the *tankist*, waving his arms. "We, the soldiers, the farmers, the people. . . ." He sounded like Norman Corwin.

At this point a burly police officer interrupted.

"Have you taken any pictures here?" he asked. He had the face of a friendly Boston Irishman.

I said I had and he asked for my "documents." He inspected my passport and my visa. The crowd had grown larger and more silent. The policeman returned the passport and saluted. "Well," he said loudly to the crowd, "he *is* a correspondent and he *has* a camera, so I guess it's all right for him to take pictures."

The crowd laughed, rather relieved, I thought. The tank officer put his arm around me and led me toward the train.

"Don't bother about fellows like that," he said, nodding toward the policeman. "He just wanted to talk to an American. You go right ahead and take pictures. The war is over."

I thanked him and we shook hands.

"One thing I don't understand," he said, tapping my Rolleiflex. "Why do you use a German camera?"

I said it was one of the best, better than any American camera. The *tankist* shook his head, disbelieving. "Your planes and tanks are so good, why can't you make the best cameras?"

The train whistle shrieked and I never had a chance to answer him, which is probably just as well. The next time I got off the train for any length of time was at Zilovno late in the afternoon. It was very hot and sticky. The porter said we had 30 or 40 minutes so I wandered around the town. It was pretty sad-looking: irregular rows of unpainted board shacks. The scattered log buildings were relatively modern and fancy. There were no paved sidewalks or streets. No attempt had been made at beautification anywhere. The local people were dressed in rags and snatches and few of them wore shoes. There was a large market place near the station where townsfolk were trying to sell odd bits of soap, old pants, sour milk, onions, spinach. A little trading was going on between them and the passengers who were offering bruised chocolates for onions, which cost four rubles a bunch.

During the afternoon I noticed for the first time that a small-boned blonde waitress in a smudged white jacket sauntered up and down the car corridors selling stewed fruit out of an oversize, beaten-up metal pail. Potential customers had to supply their own receptacles, usually tea glasses. On the payment of five rubles the girl would swish the liquid in the pail with a big dipper and dish out the compote. On other occasions she came through the train offering *pirozhkis* (meat pastries), hot soup and candies for sale.

The passengers, with a few wealthy exceptions, shunned the high-priced restaurant, ate the sausage, bread and sardines which they had lugged from Vladivostok, and supplemented this fare with purchases from villagers at stations. The villagers, in turn, crowded into the restaurant car with their accumulated savings to buy luxuries which they evidently never got in their local stores. At the stations the blonde waitress would change her beat from the car corridors to the platform to sell little pieces of unwrapped, whitish chocolate or two hard candies for five rubles. The Soviet government allows the restaurant car to charge such high prices as it helps to drain off surplus rubles, helps to prevent inflation. Servicemen and veterans who cannot afford the restaurant are taken care of in *stolovayas* maintained specially for them at most large depots. In these dining rooms the foot is hot, adequate and cheap.

At the town of Mogzan I watched what I thought was a poor woman buying six pieces of chocolate. She was certainly poorly dressed. I asked her why she paid such high prices. She glared at me, muttered phrases that I did not understand, and walked off. I tried another woman. She was more friendly and explained that there had been no sweets

93

sold in Mogzan since before the war. "There are none in the whole *rayon* (county)" she said, "not even the Party leader has had any. I know his wife," she added proudly. "I have lots of money." She fished under her skirt and pulled out a bulky wad of bills. "There are so few nice things to buy. Do you want to sell your shoes?"

At the same platform Victor Ivanovich had picked up exciting information which he rushed over to tell me. "I hear there is good ice cream at Sverdlovsk," he said, his blue eyes shining with joy.

"That's after tomorrow," I said wearily.

"*After* after tomorrow," corrected Ageev, who had just joined us.

Back in the compartment I asked Ageev if he liked discussing politics with Americans.

"Most times I do," he said. "But Americans are too much fond of arguing, especially about things which are fundamental."

"What things for example?"

"Freedom of speech. Freedom of press. The scope of criticism. I hear these things over and over."

Ballet and Air-Conditioning

Two young Red Fleet officers sauntered in to our compartment to look at my magazines. They were most surprised by the photographs of ballet in *Amerika*, by the pages on figure skating and art in *Life*. The Soviet citizen has come to expect strange and wonderful industrial products from American civilization—but ballet! art!—that's Russian terrain.

94

I asked Victor Ivanovich if he wouldn't care to show the pictures in *Amerika* to his six-year-old boy and his wife, who were traveling in our car. "No, I will tell you. They are happy to be going to Moscow. There are many things they will not have. Not yet for a while." He smiled. "You understand?"

"The Stalin Five Year Plan will give us these things," Ageev said.

The sun didn't set until very late. The car had begun to smell—a combination of old plumbing, unbathed bodies and the assorted food parcels. Our compartment was almost unbearably hot, dusty and stuffy. Facetiously, I asked Ageev if the new Five Year Plan provided air-conditioned trains for the Trans-Siberian Railroad. His face reddened and he ground out his cigarette. He was furious, the only time he was really angry with me on the entire journey.

"What for air-conditioning?" he shouted. "Our country needs anything on wheels. It's perfectly all right for you Americans to talk about air-conditioning. Your country has not been invaded three times within thirty years. Air-conditioning! Pfui!" He spat.

After a moment, he calmed down. "It is difficult for you to understand," he said softly in Russian. "Someday I will tell you the story of my life, a hard Russian life."

"I would like to hear it," I said. He never did tell me.

The sound of spitting was coming from the corridor and I peered out to investigate. The tall young *provodnik* was going up and down the rose-carpeted corridor with a glass of water clutched in his big fist. Every so often he would swig some of the water into his mouth, then bending over, he would spray it out through his lips onto the carpet.

"Makes the dust stay down," he explained to me between gulping and spraying.

Chita for Shubas

During the morning of the fifth day we arrived at Chita. The countryside had changed. The *taiga* line had receded and instead, on both sides of the tracks, there was rolling cattle land not unlike Montana. Sheep were everywhere. The city of Chita, on the left bank of the Chita River where it falls into the Amur Basin, was founded in 1825 by the Dekabrists. The Dekabrists, or Decembrists, had participated in an abortive revolt against Nicholas I in December, 1825. The Tsar had commuted their death sentences to exile in Siberia. Until the second Five Year plan the growth of Chita was slow. In 1897 there were only eleven thousand inhabitants, in 1932 only seventy-one thousand. The present population, according to Ageev, is about two hundred thousand.

Outside of Chita there were crude, reinforced log air-raid shelters not more than fifty yards from the railroad; similar ones had been visible all across Siberia. But at Chita I also saw pillboxes, no longer very carefully camouflaged by tree branches. The threat of Japanese invasion in this area had been considered great chiefly because Chita was the terminus of a spur line of the Japanese-held Chinese Eastern Railroad running north from Changchun and Harbin.

"What's Chita famous for?" I asked Vassily, the general's aide.

"Here they produce gold, lead, vodka and, best of all, *shubas*," Vassily said.

"What's a *shuba*?"

"A big, heavy, warm, wool-lined greatcoat like the Red Army wore in the cold. If the Nazis had known about *shubas*. . . . " He laughed and whacked my back.

The kiosk was sold out of the local newspaper, but I managed to buy a back issue of the *Trans-Baikal Worker* by bribing the news dealer with a cigarette. The June 8th number contained a leading article on the importance of preparing for gathering the hay. The second page was devoted almost entirely to stories about Kalinin and included a picture of his birthplace. A complaint column on the third page published a long letter from a widow who had lost her husband in the war. A collective farmer, she had four children to raise and was not receiving enough help from the local veterans' administration office. The children had to stop going to school for lack of clothes and shoes. She concluded: "I have appealed to the village Soviet and to the executive of my collective farm but nothing has been done. I feel it my duty to bring this to your attention, Comrade Editor. . . ."

The fourth and final page of the newspaper was crowded with foreign news. There were reports on the war crime trials in Nurenberg and Tokyo, the elections in Turkey and France. A dispatch from Paris stated that a town in Belgium had re-named an embankment of its river after

Generalissimo Stalin. There were two unflattering stories
about the British. An Iranian newspaper was quoted as
charging that the British had not withdrawn their troops
from Iran or from neighboring Iraq; a Tass cable from Berlin described the formation of a foreign police legion in the
British zone in Germany. This legion was to be composed
of dissatisfied émigré elements: anti-democratic Poles, Yugoslavs, and Balts who would not return to their homes. "The
Legion will have blue uniforms and carry tommy guns," the
dispatch ended.

The back pages carried an unusual amount of advertising,
all classified. There were obituaries, notices of divorces,
theatrical and motion picture showings, and educational
opportunities. The Chita State Pedagogical and Teachers
Institute was advertising for students. The Chita Technical
School offered a three months' course to untrained men and
women over eighteen and promised a salary of one hundred
and fifty rubles per month during the period of study. The
largest advertisement was headlined in black type:

WORKERS WANTED

The Chita Construction Company urgently requires more
carpenters, drivers, machinists, bricklayers, hodcarriers,
cement mixers, plumbers, and ordinary laborers.

I showed this advertisement to one of the demobilized
soldiers who was riding on top of my car. "Why wouldn't
a job here interest you?" I asked him. He curled his lips.
"This wilderness? No, thank you. I will earn more in Kharkov, even if it is destroyed. Besides," he winked, "the Ukrain-

ian girls are much more—" and he made undulating movements with his hands.

Ulan Ude, the Red Gate

At dinner time Ageev stepped up the order of vodka for
me, and after we had eaten I fell asleep. About ten that
night we arrived at Ulan Ude which means, in the Buryat
language, "Red Gate." Ulan Ude is the bilingual capital of
the Buryat-Mongolian Autonomous Republic; the schools
and newspapers use both Russian and Buryat. From the train
window I saw the huge locomotive repair shops. The city
also has a large glass works, a big meat packing plant. During the war it was known for the manufacture of a vitamin
C drink which had been originally developed in under-
nourished, besieged Leningrad. Ulan Ude turned out fifteen
thousand quarts daily of this tonic extracted from pine
needles.

On the platform I met Poppa. "I have been here before,"
he said. "In 1926 I went from Ulan Ude to Ulan Bator. Five
days down river, I think the Orkhon River. Then five days
by camel to Ulan Bator, which used to be Urga. From there
I went with a caravan to Peking."

A spindly-legged, barefooted girl sidled close to us. "Uncle,
give me some money . . . some bread. . . ." she whined.
Poppa gave her ten rubles.

He apologized: "In Shanghai I never gave beggars a
kopeck. But that child is Russian. . . ."

There were thirty or forty determined Red Army men
waiting to push aboard our train. I couldn't see any spare

99

room but they climbed on anyhow. The spaces between the
cars were long ago filled, and now the top of the train was
heavy with travelers. Local passengers were desperately grabbing onto the handrails of the cars and balancing precariously on the steps.

In the car one of the consular secretaries asked me how
I liked the Mongolians. I told him I didn't know any except
some Mongolian delegates to the Supreme Soviet who had
lived on my floor in the Metropole Hotel in Moscow during
the war. The secretary took the opportunity to tell me about
the effectiveness of the Lenin-Stalin nationalist policy.

I cut him off: "I know all about it. I made a tour of
Central Asia in 1944 with Eric Johnston and, from what I
could see, I though the Soviet government was doing an
admirable job. But I saw and heard a lot of things in China
which I did not admire."

"What's that?" The secretary slid the door of his compartment closed.

"In Manchuria the attitude of the Russians toward the
Chinese was extremely bad. They did not treat the Chinese
as equals. They often treated them with scorn, contempt."

"Perhaps just some uneducated soldiers?"

"I don't know. The Soviet commander in Mukden, General Kavtoun-Stankevich, told a group of Allied correspondents that the Chinese were dirty, that they had an inferior culture, that they were an inferior people, that. . . ."

"That is strange," the secretary broke in. "I have never
heard that. It is hard to believe."

"I found it hard to believe, but I checked. I even checked with the general's interpreter."

"*If* the general said *that*, he was wrong," said the Foreign Office man. "But did General Patton's attitude toward the Italian people represent the viewpoint of America?"

"No. Where did you learn about that?"

The Russian was pleased. "Our reports," he said. "Perhaps *War and the Working Class*."

He opened the door and I went to my compartment.

Glorious Sea

There were four or five Russians crowded into our coupe, sampling Ageev's gin and my magazines.

"Tomorrow Baikal," one said.

Ageev said to me: "My dear, you must get up. It's about five in the morning. I will tell the old man to wake you."

"What's that song about Baikal?" I asked. I had first heard the lovely old melody on the Ob River near Novosibirsk when "Mike" Kulagin, the Party boss, had sung it.

The colonel of the engineers went for his harmonica. A group of the passengers bunched together and began singing the Baikal song. I made them sing it over and over until I had all the words in Russian. Later the song was translated in Moscow, like this:

Glorious sea,
Holy Baikal!
My jolly little ship
Is an *omul* fish barrel,
Hey, move that oar!
We are nearing home.

I carried clinking chains for a long time,
I wandered in the mountains of Akatui.
An old friend helped me to escape
And the air of freedom put new strength in me.
I walked by night and I walked in daytime,
Skirting the towns, watching closely for signs of danger.
Peasant women supplied me with bread and *makhorka* I got
    from the *chaldon* boys.

Shilka and Nerchinsk frighten me no more,
The mountain police failed to overtake me.
The ravenous beasts in the thicket spared me,
The bullets of the pickets missed me.

Glorious sea,
Holy Baikal!
My good gay sail is my torn prison coat,
Hey, move that oar!
A thunderous storm is approaching.

The *omul* is a whitefish peculiar to Lake Baikal, and *chaldon* is the local name for a peasant. Shilka and Nerchinsk are the names of mining towns in Siberia where political prisoners were maltreated under the tsars. They are just east of Chita on the Trans-Siberian route, but we had gone through them at night.

At 5 A.M. the *provodnik* ambled up and down the corridor, pounding on the doors calling "Baikal! Baikal! Beautiful Baikal!" I sat up in bed and raised the window shade. The scene was a mirage: thin streaks of pre-dawn light faintly visible through the hoary mist which clung over the water. As I watched, dawn came with a rush. In a half hour the sky, except for one warm spot, was the icy blue-gray color of the lake and the shimmering water was tinted with the saffron and pink of a picture postcard sunset sky.

Lake Baikal is a scientific phenomenon that would keep Ripley happy, believe it or not, for months. Larger than Belgium, Baikal is the deepest and one of the largest fresh water inland seas in the world. Geologists believe that it was once connected with the Arctic Ocean. More than three hundred rivers and streams flow into it and only one river, the Angara, flows out.

Long before we reached the Baikal station at seven, I was up and dressed. I went out to the vestibule and the old man made me a glass of tea. I drank it standing in the doorway gazing out at the lake.

Every few minutes the train would enter a tunnel and the view would be cut off.

"There are forty-seven tunnels through the rock," the *provodnik* said. "The lake is called 'The White-haired' because of the mist you saw before."

I hummed, "Glorious Sea, Holy Baikal."

The *provodnik* said: "Do you know why the Angara is the only river that flows away from Baikal? It is a strange river, the Angara. You will see it today. She floods in the autumn instead of the spring."

I asked: "Why is the Angara the only river that flows out?"

The old man began rolling a cigarette with a corner of a newspaper. I gave him half a package of mine. He thanked me and again blessed my family.

"There is a story," he began, wetting the end of the

cigarette. He started to tell it to me, but the language was far too poetic. It had to be retold when one of the Red Fleet men could translate it for my notes. "It is a legend of May and January," the old man recounted. "Once there lived an old man with a white beard and his name was Baikal. He had a lively, lovely young wife and her name was Angara. Baikal was a jealous old man. To prevent other men from feasting their eyes on his beautiful wife he surrounded their home with high mountains. When the fog lifts completely you can see the peaks. They have snowcaps.

"But Angara was impatient and dissatisfied. She did not want to be chained; she wanted to move about, to roam freely. She dreamed of a younger, stronger lover than old Baikal. One dark Siberian night in the autumn of the year, while Baikal snored, Angara turned into a torrential river. She broke through the mountains and flooded the plain. Baikal awoke and discovered his wife was escaping. Angrily he lifted a huge cliff and hurled it in front of her path. The cliff cracked into great boulders. But Angara would not be checked. She rushed past the rocks and boulders farther and farther away from old Baikal until she at last reached the bosom of the younger, stronger lover of her dreams, Yenisei. And that, according to an old Russian tale, is why today the Angara flows so rapidly from Baikal to Yenisei."

Later, as the tracks followed the course of the Angara from Baikal Station to Irkutsk, the colonel of engineers told me there were plans to harness the Angara and create a giant hydroelectric station which would supply the whole Baikal-

Irkutsk area with cheap power. "The Angara and other rivers around here have a waterpower potential of twenty million kilowatts," he said. (The TVA had a 2,265,982 kilowatt capacity at the end of 1945.)

Near the Baikal station, soldiers from the train stripped and washed themselves along the rocky shores of the lake. The water was cold and transparent. A few fishermen were just setting off in their skiffs, poling away from the shallow water.

Here for the first time on the trip three or four of the other passengers produced cameras and snapped pictures.

Vassily was watching me take my pictures. He was buying fish.

"You know," he said, "I think now I met you in Tokyo. Are you acquainted with Dennis McEvoy?"

"Of the *Reader's Digest?*"

"Yes. He speaks very good Russian. I think I met you once when I was drinking with McEvoy."

"Maybe so."

"Would you take my picture?"

I told him I would. I posed him against the International car. The colonel of engineers saw me and placed himself in the picture.

I didn't care, but the aide wasn't too pleased. He said nothing, only glared.

After we left the Baikal station there were occasional glimpses of the snowcapped Sayan mountain range. On the way to Irkutsk, Ageev and Victor Ivanovich asked me questions about the cost of living in America. How did it compare to Moscow? To Shanghai? Was it going up or down? I explained that prices were going up, wages were going up, but that the former were outdistancing the latter. It is just as difficult trying to translate the way a "free" economy works to a Russian as it is explaining the Soviet price structure to a citizen of the capitalist world.

"American economy expanded and increased many times during the war," Ageev said. "Why isn't there a great amount of goods?" I mentioned retooling, reconversion and the accumulated wartime savings by the workers. He was not satisfied with my explanations. And neither was I.

Irkutsk, Old and New

Irkutsk has two stations: one in the old section, one in the new. It is a transportation and trading center almost in the middle of the Vladivostok-Moscow span. The town was built by the Cossacks in 1652 near the confluence of the Irkut and Angara Rivers about forty miles west of Lake Baikal. By the end of the seventeenth century the first trade caravans laden with Russian furs were leaving Irkutsk for China and returning with fine silks. Before the Revolution thousands of Bolsheviks were exiled to the Irkutsk area including Kuibyshev, Frunze and Stalin. During the postrevolutionary intervention period the city, with a population of about one hundred thousand, was occupied by Czech troops.

At the outbreak of the last war Irkutsk had 250,000 inhabitants, a big machine tool plant, leather, soap, shoe and macaroni factories and a power station. During the war, fac-

tories from the Ukraine were brought to Irkutsk because of
its closeness to transportation and to the coal of Cheremkhovo, the largest fields in the Far East, with estimated reserves of one hundred billion tons.

The day's newspaper which I bought at Irkutsk was called
The East Siberian Pravda. The front-page story listed the
standings of the tractor brigades as an American journal
might box the standings of major league baseball teams. The
leading editorial analyzed the reasons for the bad work of
the Machine Tractor Stations (MTS): inefficient management, poor planning, need for training, failure to care for
equipment and lack of understanding of the problem of the
harvest. The Soviet enthusiasm for self-criticism, restrained
during the war years, was burgeoning forth again.

On the second page there were more features on Kalinin's
career including a picture of a house where he had resided
in 1909.

The Irkutsk paper was livelier than those I had read in
Vladivostok, Khabarovsk or Chita. On page three was an interesting feature called FIGURES AND FACTS from 1939
to 1945, and another headlined WILL BE BUILT. The
general-in-pajamas had his aide bring him a paper. He turned
immediately to page four, which is devoted to foreign news.
If the general read it carefully and believed what he read,
he was certain that German troops were training in the
British zone for a reason unfriendly to the U.S.S.R. Other
dispatches were less angled: reports of a bread ration cut in
Belgium, a republican demonstration in Rome, a monarchist
rally in Naples, a session of the Norwegian Communist party,

the trial at Nurenberg, and the English Labor party Conference's rejection of a unity bid from the Communists.

The Irkutsk advertising columns were similar in kind to those in the Chita paper. The Irkutsk School for Railroad Workers offered courses with stipends and food allotments according to the applicant's ability in passing examinations in Russian, dictation, mathematics and the Constitution of the U.S.S.R. A private *artel* announced it was open for business: glasses and mirrors repaired, books bound, pictures framed, musical instruments fixed.

Siberia: Giant with Thyroid

The passing of Irkutsk brought me to one of the pencil marks I had made on my map. It has been aptly said that Siberia, like Gaul, may be divided into three parts: far eastern Siberia, stretching from the Pacific Coast to Lake Baikal; central Siberia, from the Irkutsk region westward to Novosibirsk; and western Siberia, extending westward from Novosibirsk to the Urals. I opened my notebook and tried to sum up a few impressions of the Soviet Far East. All that I remembered learning about Siberia in school was that it was a vast, far off, very cold country inhabited by exiles. There are still exiles in the Far East; it is still vast and very cold. But it is hardly "far off." Khabarovsk is as close to Seattle as New York is. Soviet Far East airports are only a day's flight from Oregon and Washington and California.

Glancing back over my notes, I found that I had been unconsciously comparing Siberia to America, forgetting that

Siberia was just emerging from economic wilderness, that it was still raw, rough, unfinished, pioneer. Siberia is America as it was one hundred years ago; but it won't require one hundred years to catch up. It is growing like an unruly young giant with a surplus of thyroid. With its energies channelized and directed, Siberia can catch up in thirty, forty or fifty years. I put that in my notebook and then I added: "Provided there is peace." I underlined it.

PART III

5,800 MILES ON THE TRANS-SIBERIAN
B. Irkutsk to Moscow

On this day, the sixth, and the half-way point of the trip, the greatest changes in terrain occurred. The rolling plains and valleys were patterned with tilled fields. The earth was darker and richer, the foliage fuller, the trees taller and more infrequent. An occasional whitewashed house sparkled in the unpainted villages and the peasants who milled around the station platforms at train time had more produce to sell. Eggs, chickens, cucumbers, radishes, nuts and berries were plentiful, and there was even bread and sour milk. Prices were much lower than they had been during the war when I had made the Baku-Moscow trip. Eggs, hard-boiled, were now four and five rubles apiece compared to twelve and fifteen. A roasted chicken cost over two hundred rubles in 1943-1944, and the farmers preferred to have sweets or other goods instead of currency. Now the ruble was definitely in demand and better-fed chickens were going for sixty or seventy rubles.

110

Between Irkutsk and Cheremkhovo we paused at a way station called Polovina, which means "half." Polovina marked the spot where the two gangs of railroaders working from east and west joined tracks and completed the Trans-Siberian route in 1896. At Cheremkhovo, the coal center, the train went past a big new Japanese detention camp. The prisoners of war were toiling in the nearby fields almost without guards, but I doubt if they could have gotten very far in an attempted escape.

Three brawny civilians who looked like coal miners tried to climb atop our car. The old *provodnik* chased them off. "This is a deluxe car," he said, brandishing his signal flag, "and even our roof is reserved for our glorious demobilized soldiers." The three men laughed and moved on to another car. At another stop two drunks tried to barge in. When he had blocked their way the old man turned to me and said, "Typically Russian. Only Russians act that way. Drunk, not tidy, full of fight." I protested that Americans could behave exactly the same way. The *provodnik* refused to believe me. "Americans are gentlemen," he said. "We Russians are only big boys not very long away from the cowsheds."

At Kansk the next afternoon there was an encouraging signboard. It read: To Moscow—4,368 kilometers; To Vladivostok—4,980. For the first time I had a secure feeling that we were inching toward our destination.

Ageev felt more cheerful, too. After dinner he mentioned quite casually that he had been at Teheran during the Big Three meeting in 1943.

"It was just by chance," he said, "I was not a member of the staff."

He had seen the Big Three and had been greatly impressed. "Roosevelt is needed now more than I can say," he said. "We believed he was our friend. We trusted him. I do not know this Truman, but he does not seem strong enough to oppose the will of your reactionary forces."

I told Ageev, in English, the two Teheran jokes that I know. Stalin was involved in both of them. Ageev was politely amused. He translated them into Russian for Victor Ivanovich, who was not amused at all.

"I will tell you story about Foreign Ministers' conference," Ageev said. "Translators of Mr. Byrnes and Mr. Molotov argue about which country has more freedom, my country or yours. Translator of Mr. Byrnes is positive that he has more freedom. He tells translator of Mr. Molotov, 'Why, I can go up to Mr. Byrnes and say to him Mr. Byrnes, your policy on Russia is terrible, and he will slap me on my back and be very friendly.' Translator of Mr. Molotov is surprised. 'What is so unusual about that?' he demands. 'I can go up to Mr. Molotov and say to him, Mr. Byrnes' policy on Russia is terrible, and he will slap me on back and be very friendly.'"

I laughed and said that story was just as true as it was funny.

"You like that joke?" asked Ageev. "All right, I will tell you one secret. That was American joke, not Russian. One American man in Shanghai told me that."

"Do *you* think it's funny?"

VLADIVOSTOK

n the deck of the *Smolny* a group of
ussian children from Shanghai pose
r a picture (*above*). Their parents
ve recently acquired Soviet citizen-
ip. The girl in the second row, far
ft, is half Chinese. *Right:* first sight
Vladivostok from the *Smolny*. The
yage took six days but new vessels
ill do it in about three.

Zolotoi Rog (Golden Horn) Harbor is four miles long, a mile wide. In the winter

Vladivostok's main market is a busy trading center from early morning to late at night. Prices on rationed goods in stores are fixed but not in this bazaar.

Vladivostok's busiest corner is the intersection of 25th of October and Le[n]
Streets. Above the *gastronom* (grocery) is the *Zolotoi Rog,* the city's only nightcl[u]

Russian Orthodox Church, only one in
area, is this white frame structure.

Chelyuskin Hotel is Vladivostok's b[e]
The jeep at the curb is U. S. Lend-Lea[se]

ading department store, on Lenin Street, was built before the Revolution. It is
lassic example of pre-Soviet Russian architecture which one still sees in Siberia.

w Five Year Plan advertised on main
eet depicts shoe production rise.

Finest movie house, *Oussouri,* is showing a prewar U. S. musical, *Great Waltz.*

Vladivostok Officers' Naval Training School turns out new leaders for the Pacific Fleet after four-year course. Most famous Red Fleet school is located in Leningrad

Barracks which housed United States intervention forces under General W. S. Graves in 1919 are now utilized by the Red Army for an infantry training school

Second River Concentration Camp, just recently enlarged, is said to be filled with Russian political prisoners. Soviet authorities refused to affirm or deny this.

Entrance to a small ship repair plant near Vladivostok's Diomedes Bay is decorated by patriotic slogans. An armed guard in hut (right) checks all visitors and workers.

Vladivostok's only new housing project is reserved for naval officers and their families. The cable wire being strung is marked "product of Western Electric."

Rooming facilities are so crowded in the port city that Red Army men who are on temporary duty live in this tent encampment on the outskirts of Vladivostok.

rnate new pink stucco sanatorium for Soviet Pacific Fleet is located near the
ore front at Okeanskaya, a few miles from the main naval base at Vladivostok.

On Sundays Vladivostokians come to the bathing beach at the 19th Kilometer on the suburban train. They swim and boat in the quiet waters along the Amur River Gulf

A couple of kids watch sailors trying their luck in a shooting gallery at the beach. There are no prizes for accuracy. These tars were good shots, hit the bull's-eye consistently

Two-piece bathing suits, as worn by these Soviet belles, are the rage. They also require less material. Nude swimming is now taboo, but bathers can change clothes behind bushes.

The beach also has a jazz band. Sailors often dance together but authorities frown on the custom. Cost of drinks and amusements was low and everyone seemed to have fun.

TRANS-SIBERIAN

Our old, Russian-built, flower-festooned locomotive averaged 20-miles an hour.

The fare for my ticket in this International car was slightly more than $125.

At some stations townspeople would besiege the restaurant car in an attempt to buy cake, rolls, wine and other luxuries still unavailable in their store

Passengers who rode on the steps of my car and the one behind it bought their food from peasants without getting down. They were afraid to lose their places.

Julie, the flirt, liked black dresses and scallions. The old porter grins at her.

Dmitri, an ex-flier, was on his way home to marry after six years in the army

The colonel of engineers and Vassily, the general's aide, pose near the car.

A Red Army general enroute from Tokyo wore these Jap pajamas on train

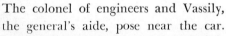

habarovsk was the first big stop. On the Amur River, it is the capital of a terri-
ry with an area of 450,000 square miles and a population of about 2,000,000.

utside the station families live while waiting for trains westward or for shelter
. Khabarovsk. The city's population swelled from 200,000 to 300,000 during war.

Approaching Lake Baikal the train went through a series of tunnels in the roc
like the one in the upper center. Most trees in this hilly section are evergree

At Baikal station the usual posters hail the Red Army. The Soviet Academy
Sciences has a research outpost here studying flora and fauna around the la

Early in the morning a fisherman poles out into Baikal, the earth's deepest fresh-water sea. In the lake there are mammal-type fish which are fifty per cent fat.

Zilovno is a typical Siberian town. The roads are unpaved, the wooden houses

stalls (right) where peasants sold local foods to passengers at reasonable prices.

This peasant woman with her water buckets paused to watch the train. Af
Irkutsk the look of the land changed and birches replaced stunted evergree

ear Novosibirsk herds of beef cattle grazed along the tracks. Passengers told me
nat local breeds were Holstein, Simmenthaler, Yaroslav and Kholmogory.

NOVOSIBIRSK In Siberia's Chicago this girl in boots sold bouquet for a few rubles. She was evacuated from Leningrad

Novosibirsk's station, the largest and finest in the U.S.S.R., was completed in 1943. Millions of refugees from the west passed through here during the war years.

A barefoot boy awaits a train while a man peruses *Komsomolskaya Pravda*.

A little boy in an Uzbek scullcap plays boats in a puddle on the platform.

Novosibirsk's suburbs on the western bank of the Ob River are booming with newly built apartments and factories. City is a big plane manufacturing center.

The Trans-Siberian Express became overcrowded and hardy travelers climbed on top of cars. Most passengers, inside and out, were demobilized servicemen.

Demobilized army men ride home in box-cars wearing their decorations.

At Kungur I was detained by police for photographing this Lenin statue.

In the Urals food became plentiful and more varied while the prices declined.

I also photographed these people, and they did not like the idea very much

At the city of Kirov passengers lined up to procure boiling water for tea. The children on the doorstep asked for candy. They said they were war orphans.

Compared to a Siberian town, this place west of the Urals has an air of planning and permanence. This Park of Culture and Rest is in the center of the town.

Dining halls where servicemen can eat cheaply are maintained at most depots.

But washroom facilities are limited and many clean up at the water tower

MOSCOW After drab Siberia, the wide boulevards of the capital and the modern Council of Ministers building are impressive.

New development along the Moscow River banks will make this residential area one of the city's finest. Similar apartments were built for Red Army generals.

This workers' apartment house had seven stories built before the war and is now being finished with two more. Moscow's room shortage is still extremely serious.

The Bolshoi Theatre has been refurbished inside and out. Latest interior decorator removed the slogan "Workers of the World, Unite!" from the proscenium.

verdlovsk Square is washed daily by water trucks. The tall structure is the Moskva Iotel, the city's best, reserved for Soviet citizens and visitors like Earl Browder.

Unawed by the dominating spires of the Kremlin, kids (left) plunge into the

Ageev shrugged. "It is not funniest story I have ever heard, but politically it is not so bad as most American jokes about Russians."

Those Siberian Mines

Between Kansk and Krasnoyarsk I had my first talk with Zamenchek, the inspector of mines. I began it by telling him that I had been in Fushun, Manchuria, and had inspected there the largest open-face coal mine in the world. At the time it had been operated and managed by a group of Soviet engineers. Shortly afterward the Chinese Nationalists kicked them out. The inspector questioned me concerning the production figures, the mine's potential yield and what the present plans were for its development. He ignored any political implications on the Soviet-Chinese dispute over management.

"The new Five Year Plan," he said, "provides for the opening of new coal fields in Siberia which will make this area self-sufficient. No longer need we depend on the Donbas."

"How are conditions in the Siberian mines now? They are still notorious throughout the world as hell-holes because of the Siberian legends."

"I can tell you conditions are not good. Of course, you understand they do not compare with conditions under the tsars. It is only that during the war the equipment was not repaired properly, the men worked very long hours; nobody gave enough attention to housing and sanitation and safety measures. The entire emphasis was on production. To win the war was the chief goal. Now everyone expects everything

113

to be done at once, and we are experiencing many difficulties. There is now a whole new system of priorities. During the war everything was planned from above by the government. Now, within the big plan, the month to month ordering of supplies, getting dates and methods of delivery are decided by regional boards."

"What's being done to improve things?"

"Men like myself are sent out to help reorganize. The mines are really not so poorly off. We keep a fairly close eye on the big ones from Moscow. But the factory situation is bad, especially in those which have reconverted to consumer products."

"Why?"

"Change of procedure again. When they were manufacturing war materials, Moscow organized everything for them —ordered supplies, tended to deliveries, set prices. Now they must make competitive goods of high quality."

"Competitive? I should think the demand for consumer goods is so great that everything would sell."

"No. The state stores which are the main distributors for a certain kind of glove, as an example, will go to several factories to price them. If one factory makes a good glove for a moderate price and another a poor glove at a higher price, the first factory will get the order and the second one will be investigated."

"Is there any graft in Soviet industry?"

Zamenchek was not as outraged as I thought he would be. If I had asked an American Russophile the same question he might have exploded with anger. The inspector said:

"During the war, almost none. Now some certain people are grabbing. There will have to be closer check-ups. One is going on now, in fact."

I told him that the Chinese Communists in Manchuria favored placing certain industries in the hands of private capital because they felt government officials were less efficient and more apt to take "squeeze."

"That's China," said the inspector. "What can you expect from the Chinese?"

"You sound just like an American business man, "I told him, a little disgusted. He was pleased.

Krasnoyarsk and Tannu Tuva

About five in the afternoon the train crawled through the eastern suburbs of Krasnoyarsk. For miles it seemed like nothing more than the graveyard for hundreds of ancient or wrecked locomotives. Before crossing the Yenisei, we had a look at the city's new section, almost entirely built up within the past fifteen years. The river itself did not have the romantic appearance suited to Angara's strong young lover. It was wide and sluggish, the color of bread mold. It rises in Outer Mongolia, empties into the Arctic Ocean 2,950 miles away.

The older part of the city on the western bank of the Yenisei had evidently not changed much in past decades. The backbone of the residential area was still the same type of *izba* log hut as the one in which Lenin and Krupskaya spent their honeymoon-in-exile. There were more *izbas* and here and there large apartment houses to take care of the sharp rises in population. Fifty years ago Krasnoyarsk had a population of twenty-five thousand, most of them political prisoners. Today the city is in the three hundred thousand class.

Olga Belikovsky, the girl from Birobidzhan, got off the train with a valise, a wicker hamper held together with cord, and a bundle tied up in a blanket.

"I am a little scared," she said, as she stood there on the platform gazing at the station. "This is the first time I have been away from Birobidzhan since I was four years old."

"What do you do right now?"

"I think I must telephone the institute where I will study, and they will arrange everything."

She was silent for a minute and then she said slowly, "I hope many American correspondents will come to see Birobidzhan soon. You will see, if we have peace for a long time, life will not be so bad for us. Do you think there will be peace for a long time?"

I said I certainly hoped so but that it depended a good deal on mutual understanding.

"My father thinks that people in the United States have too many good things to understand other people who have less. Well, I must go. No, please, I can carry these without trouble. You know you are the first American I have ever met. Also the first foreigner. Except for those who are now Soviet citizens in Birobidzhan." I held out my hand. Instead of shaking it, Olga saluted, picked up her gear and marched into the station.

At Krasnoyarsk I made inquiries about the Republic of

Tannu Tuva, whose independence had been recognized by the Soviets in 1918. In Shanghai an UNRRA official had suggested that I have a look at Tuva. I thought she had invented the name. But she brought out a recent map and showed me this small Mongolian country (population 65,000) several hundred miles south of Krasnoyarsk.

"I want to go there someday," she said. "Find out what you can for me."

Nobody that I asked could tell me very much about Tannu Tuva at Krasnoyarsk. In Moscow I made further inquiries. If that UNRRA official ever reads these lines, she can forget about going to the Republic of Tannu Tuva. It may exist on her map, but it is no more as an independent state. Although no official pronouncement had been made, at the session of the Russian Supreme Soviet in Moscow last June two delegates showed up from the Tannu Tuva *oblast* (region) of the Russian Republic.

More recently fifty thousand Tuvinians wrote a letter to Generalissimo Stalin which was published in the Soviet press. They expressed their thanks because Russia had provided them with the opportunity "to bypass the capitalistic path" and promised to turn their country "into one of the blooming corners of the great Soviet Union."

At Krasnoyarsk the locomotive and cars were checked and greased. Most of the workers employed on the job were barefooted women. The majority of the porters and conductors on our train were women, and the restaurant was an all-female operation, including the manager.

117

A little boy begging bread approached a group of us standing at the car steps. "Make him sing or dance first," suggested Julie, the flirt. The idea was seconded. In a hoarse voice the little boy sang a newly popular ditty called "We drink for Stalin." When he had finished there was applause, and the general-in-pajamas gave the dirty urchin half a loaf of black bread.

Julie asked me to take her picture and I promised to do it the next day at Novosibirsk if the light was good. She continued to stroll only with Vassily and to flirt with everyone else. Despite the hot spells and the dirt she wore an array of low-cut, slightly shiny black dresses, ranging from lace to velvet and taffeta. These gowns renewed my suspicion that she was on the stage and not in the post office. She also wore a heavy, heady scent. Ageev thought she probably bathed in the stuff daily. Once he asked her the name of the perfume. She said it was called "Wait For Me," after the popular sentimental wartime ballad by Konstantin Simonov.

Nothing Ever Changes

Trouble and almost freezing weather featured the eighth day. The morning began as usual with all the amenities in Russian. We ran through the same patter routine daily. Ageev, his head propped up on one arm, greeted me, "Good morning, my dear, how did you sleep last night?"

"Strongly. And you?"

"So, so. Well, what do we do today?"

"What do you suggest?"

"First, I think maybe we eat a little. . . ."

118

"Good."

"Then read a little, then perhaps sleep a little, then eat a little, then read a little, then perhaps some walking?"

"Very good."

The trouble started before we were dressed. Hooligans had smashed the two car windows at 8 A.M. This upset the *provodniks*. By midday they were sufficiently quieted down so that they both fell asleep. In the excitement they had failed to clean up anything but the fragments of glass. A railroad inspector boarded the car shortly after noon, found both porters snoozing and the compartments full of unswept breakfast leftovers. The inspector, a saucer-eyed, string bean of a fellow, with a nervous Chekhov manner threw the whole car into a turmoil. He lectured the two porters so loudly that everyone could hear. Scolding them, he invoked the Great Patriotic War, the valor of Russian troops and even public opinion in America.

"I am told there is in your car a foreigner, an American. How will it be if he goes back to Washington and tells everybody that Russians live like pigs, that Russian railroads are operated by such sleeping champions?"

The inspector was somewhat mollified when the general and the Party functionary offered him a drink of Japanese whiskey and told him that the two porters actually worked very well.

Ageev and I were enjoying our late and leisurely breakfast during this outburst when Julie, the fleshy postmistress, appeared like an Amazon's statue in our doorway.

"You do not eat enough," she said to me sternly, batting

her eyelids. "You are too thin. If you ate more, you'd be strong like I am."

I winked at Ageev. Julie intercepted the signal. "You don't want to look like me? You don't think I am attractive?" She was really agonized.

"You are terrific," I said in English. "If you could sing you'd be the Russian Kate Smith." She did not understand. Ageev translated, using an adjective for "terrific" that I did not know. It pleased Julie. She sat down next to me and peppered me with questions about my age, my wife, my children. I showed her snapshots of my family.

"They are not well-fed, either," was her only comment. "They could not live through a Siberian winter."

"Or a summer either," I said, putting on my heaviest sweater. All the passengers that day went around wrapped up in their warmest garments. That is, all except the general, who put on flannels under his sky blue pajamas. I know this because Vassily brought in the woolies and showed them to me. "*Americanski*," he announced proudly. "Feel how soft. From your PX."

"I wish I had a pair," I said.

Before he left the train, the saucer-eyed inspector checked everyone's ticket. He discovered two demobilized soldiers riding in the vestibule without tickets and insisted that they get off. Surreptitiously they boarded another car, walked along the roof, resumed their places in our vestibule after the inspector debarked.

I told Poppa about this incident.

"You could always ride for free in Russian trains," he recalled. "Many a time I had rides without paying. Russians have always enjoyed doing things like that even when they have the money to pay. That will never change."

"You can't change human nature. That's the old cry against Marxist society."

"You can, a little. I have changed some of my views. And Marxist society has changed some of its views, too. I can do a lot of things in Russia today that I couldn't do in 1925 and 1926 when I left."

"What, for example?"

"Never mind," Poppa said, "plenty of things. I can go to church, but I do not want to. I can own a *dacha* in the country. I do not want to. Plenty of things. I might not have talked to foreigners twenty years ago. I do now because I want to."

"Maybe that's because you've lived in America and China."

"Maybe," said Poppa, "but you do not see anyone stopping me, do you?"

Novosibirsk, Siberia's Chicago

An hour before Novosibirsk a girl got on the train to take cables and telegrams. I sent one off to Moscow which never arrived.

Novosibirsk, the junction center of the Trans-Siberian and the Turk-Sib railways, surprised me again. It surprised me the first time in 1944 by its vitality, its size, its industrial development. In the intervening two years I had talked and written about the "Chicago" of the Soviet Union, but in my mind's eye I had not pictured it as overgrown as it actually is. The huge railroad station, the largest and best in the Soviet Union, was typical of the city. Something was happening in every corner. Books, newspapers, ice cream, souvenirs were being sold. Several lunchrooms open. Freshly painted slogans on the wall. Special service bureaus for soldiers and veterans. People moving to and fro briskly and with purpose. Trains arriving and departing according to the giant schedule board hung in the main concourse.

The civilians were a little better dressed; the soldiers held themselves a little straighter; the officers were snappier. We spent over an hour in the station and three or four of the new Soviet citizens went into one of the restaurants and had a meal. I met them when they came out, and for the first time on the trip I saw the "light" shining in their eyes.

"A fine meal," they said. "Good service. Reasonable prices. Clean tablecloths. This is quite a town, eh?"

Poking around the platform taking pictures, I saw the two air corps majors from Korea. It seemed months since I had talked with them in the restaurant car. The blond, round one, Glubov, was waving a telegram.

"This is bad," he said, after greeting me. "I have been ordered back."

"To Korea?"

"No, to the Vladivostok area. It is signed by Marshal Meretskov."

"How can they do that to you? I thought you were returning to civilian life."

"I thought so, too, but technically I am still in the army for another month."

"Will you be able to fly or is it another ten days back on the train?"

"I will make application to fly. With this," he fluttered the telegram, "I think I can fly."

Frezhenko said: "I will miss him."

"Does the marshal give any reason for ordering your return?" I asked.

They both shook their heads. "Marshals do not need reasons," Frezhenko muttered.

I presented Glubov with all the Russian reading material I had and several packs of cigarettes.

Thanking me, he said, "When I hear the American army song I will think of you."

"What American army song?"

"Surely you must know it." He began to hum and Frezhenko sang the words in Russian. It was "There's a Tavern in the Town."

"Where did you learn that? And who told you it was the American army song?"

"It is," said Frezhenko, curtly. "We learned it at Poltava during the war from your fliers."

"It's a fine, merry song," said Glubov.

Frezhenko said: "Ukrainian songs are better." As boastful as Russians are, Ukrainians are more so. They are, as Ed Angly of the Chicago *Sun* pointed out to the Russians on many occasions, the Texans of the Soviet Union. The Ukrainians think they sing, love, eat, shoot, ride, fight and fly better than anybody else, and they are probably right.

When Julie descended upon me, the majors shook hands quickly and fled. I took Julie's picture. She gave me her address in Vladivostok.

"I will only be in Moscow a week or ten days," she said, "but if you are ever in Vladivostok, don't forget Julie . . ."

"If I'm ever in Vladivostok. . . ." I promised.

When the train left the Novosibirsk station, it moved slower than its accustomed 20-mile-an-hour pace. This gave me a chance to stand in the doorway of the car and make pictures of the countryside. Fat, glossy-skinned cattle grazed peacefully along the rich land beyond the west bank of the Ob River. Further on we chugged past a booming new factory suburb which I had never seen nor heard about before. There were new power and cement plants, soap and candy factories, and large, square, red brick apartment houses which were still being built. I wondered if Novosibirsk's three-quarters of a million people were as hard pressed for living space as in 1944. Then many had to be content in dugouts, lean-to's, temporary barracks and tents.

One of Russia's scientific greats, Professor Dmitri Ivanovich Mendeleyev, predicted at the turn of the century that "the center of gravity of Russia's population will eventually be in the neighborhood of Omsk." Barring atomic disasters, this probably won't come true within the next generation. But the Soviets do propose that at the conclusion of the next two Five Year Plans, Omsk and Novosibirsk will be the center of gravity for Russia's heavy industry.

Bottoms Up!

We went through Omsk the next morning, and I didn't see any of it. Earlier in the trip I had shown Ageev my passport. Reading it, he noted that I had a birthday on June 18th and immediately made plans for a "big holiday." On that morning I was awakened by a frightened three-year-old girl from the next compartment who presented me with a large and lovely bunch of very red radishes. Then Victor Ivanovich came in with a dozen white eggs and kissed me on both cheeks. The alcohol toasts got under way at breakfast and lasted until after dinner when I passed out. I awoke at ten in the evening with a headache.

The compartment was strewn with champagne bottles. I could not figure that out. I recalled drinking vodka, wine and cognac.

The postmistress came in and changed the cold wet towel on my aching forehead. Observing that I was not only alive, but awake, she called Ageev.

"How did these champagne bottles get here?" I demanded.

"Why, we drank them, my dear," said Ageev, gently.

"Did I drink any?"

"Certainly," said Julie, "you drank my health. You drank almost a full bottle for American-Soviet friendship."

Ageev nodded.

"How do you feel?" he asked.

"Terrible."

He wagged his head dolefully. "You know, my dear, you really should not drink. You cannot. You have no capacity."

I said: "I never want another drink."

"Good. I will get you a glass of tea now." Ageev disappeared.

On a twelve-day train trip a man who, like myself, cannot drink, at least has the consolation of being able to blot out one whole day. I was not conscious enough to register much of what was going on around me until we reached Sverdlovsk, the next morning. In that way I slept through Omsk, Isil Kul, Petrapavlovsk, Kurgan, Kopetsk and Chelyabinsk. Ageev said they were charming towns and that I had missed dozens of excellent pictures.

"The light was bad," I said.

He was surprised. "So it was. But how did you know? Or was everything black? You really shouldn't drink, my dear."

Looking over the map of the territory we had covered during my blackout, I was struck by one thing. In Moscow during the war foreigners invariably thought of the Urals as the "eastern" part of Russia. But traveling from the Far East, one does not reach the foothills of the Urals until the ninth day!

Sverdlovsk and the Urals

The Urals is the name applied to the mineral-rich belt of land, thirty-one to ninety-three miles from east to west, 1,550 miles from north to south, which divides Asia and Europe. The Ural Mountains, from which the region derives its appellation and fame, are not a very lofty range. Around Sverdlovsk, the center of the belt, they are no more than a thousand feet in height. However, the Urals more than make up in lavish content what they lack in physical grandeur. Among the minerals and natural resources there is iron ore, gold, platinum, cobalt, manganese, oil, nickel, chromites, asbestos, phosphorites and, according to recent reports, uranium.

Sverdlovsk, founded in 1721 as Ekaterinburg, is the largest city (population seven hundred thousand) in the Urals although Magnitogorsk and Chelyabinsk are more important industrially.

"This is a fine city," Victor Ivanovich said to me. "You should see it."

I told him I had been in Sverdlovsk before.

"I saw the spot where the last czar, Nicholas II, and his family were shot."

Victor Ivanovich was not interested. "Here is where they make machines which make machines," he said. "That is what is so important about Sverdlovsk."

At Kungur, a few hours out of Sverdlovsk, I had another brush with the police. I was photographing a statue of Lenin, the familiar one with the hand outstretched, when a member of the security police ordered me to close my camera. He asked me what I was doing in Kungur. I explained that I was a passenger on the Trans-Siberian train.

We went into my coupe. I showed him my passport, my visa, and the customs officer's written acknowledgment of my camera. The policeman appeared unmoved.

"I will take your film," he said.

At that moment four of my fellow passengers bunched into the corridor outside the door: Ageev, one of the consular officials, the two Red Fleet men.

"What's the trouble?" demanded Ageev.

The policeman was surprised. "This man has a camera. He has taken photographs in the station. That is against regulations."

"Do not be foolish," Ageev replied. "This man is a correspondent, an American. He came to our country with his camera quite openly. He was permitted to bring it with him. He is producing a story about this trip. Why shouldn't he take pictures? What's so critical or so secret about this station? He has taken pictures for ten days. What right have you to stop him?"

The policeman had an answer on his lips when one of the Red Fleet officers spoke: "Please do not forget that the war is over. This correspondent is our friend."

I asked the policeman, "What's your family name, please?"

He did not reply. He returned my passport, saluted and pushed his way out of the corridor. The navy men chortled as school kids would after pulling off a great prank. I thanked my companions.

"*Neechevo*," Ageev said, "go take more pictures."

Molotov Is Perm

Several hours later we halted at Molotov. At least it said Molotov on the map and on the timetable but the signs at the railroad station read "Perm" despite the fact the city's name was officially changed years ago. At Molotov I saw the first electric trains I had seen in Russia, except for the Moscow suburban lines.

"Where do they go?" I asked a stationmaster. Only a Russian could be so delightfully vague about such a definite thing as a railroad.

"Probably to Chusovoi, perhaps to Nizhni Tagil," he said, cracking sunflower seeds between his teeth.

Near the platform a gift shop sold colorful children's books, chessmen, wax carvings of Bolshevik busts, wooden toys and animals, playing cards, fountain pens, pencils and magazines. The Stakhanovite worker from the Vladivostok shipyards who was traveling in my car went in and came forth with at least one sample of everything that was for sale. He probably figured his purchases would keep his child happy until they changed trains at Moscow for the Caucasus.

Since Novosibirsk the amount of train traffic had increased noticeably. The commodities transported always appeared to be the same three staples: lumber, coal and men. They were all shipped in boxcars. The men, demobilized soldiers returning to their homes in the east, were in the best of spirits. Passing the other way they cheered and waved to us. At stations they accepted cigarettes, spoke with hope and zeal about their own and Russia's future, made cracks about America's "atomic diplomacy," inquired after Eisenhower's health and invited me to take their pictures.

The early evening was lovely, and I rode on the doorstep of the car after the train left Molotov. In the long dusk of the June evening the peasants were working hard. Barefooted boys were driving the cattle back from the pastures. After a full day on the collective farm, farmers were busily cultivating their own patches. Most of them were women and children.

Dress from New York

For no apparent reason, the train paused alongside a vegetable farm between Molotov and Kirov. A pretty girl in a brown muslin dress stepped carefully between rows of spinach, cabbage and radishes. She watered them with a drinking dipper which she filled from a bucket. I jumped off the train, went over to the truck garden and asked the girl for a drink of water.

"This is not boiled," she said in Russian, indicating the bucket. "But back there," she pointed "is very good well water. Are you a Czech?"

I thanked her and said I was an American. She smiled. "I thank you. This dress, my shoes, my mother's winter overcoat were given to us by the American Relief Society (Russian War Relief). Where is your home?"

"New York."

"That is where this dress comes from."

I had the drink of water and several other passengers followed my example. I returned to talk with the girl in the brown muslin dress. Her name was Tania Ivanovna; she was twenty-three and her two brothers and her fiancé had been killed in the war. "We are not certain yet that Vladimir Ivanovich—that's my younger brother—is dead. He is only missing. But we say he is dead. It is better that way. Did you lose any of your family in the war?"

I had not, I said, but I had lost good friends.

"Do you like Americans?" I asked.

"Of course, very much."

"Do you read a newspaper? Do you have a radio?"

She shook her head, rather puzzled by my questions.

"I was going to the *technicum* in 1941," she told me when I questioned her further. "That was near Kirov. But when my brothers went into the army, I was needed to work here. I work eight hours—from eight to four—at the Red October Collective over that way. We have a thousand acres for seventy-one families. At four I come home and eat with my mother and my grandfather. Then we work in our little garden here."

"Do you have enough to eat?"

"Yes, we even sell extra vegetables or trade for bread or for tobacco for the old man. We have a cow. We had two but one died. This year if crops are good, we will have a sow and some pigs."

"Have you bought any government bonds with your savings?"

"The money we will receive because of my brothers we will subscribe to bonds."

"Are you a member of the Party or the Young Communist League?"

"Oh, no."

"Why not?"

Tania stooped down and began yanking up weeds. "I do not know enough," she said. "Besides my father is not here."

"Where is he?"

The train whistle sounded.

She pulled out a handful of weed roots and then tamped down the earth around the hole. "He is working in the East, in the North at Magadan."

The train lurched into movement and so did I. When I climbed aboard, the old *provodnik* scolded me. "You are too close to Moscow now to miss the train. There will be many beautiful girls in Moscow to talk to you, much more pretty than that one." He was right, but none of them could tell me what Tania's father Ivan was doing in Magadan and why he went there.

Kirov was passed at five the next morning, long before Ageev and I arose. Since eggs were plentiful at the stations, we had them regularly for breakfast. I normally eat only two, but Ageev wouldn't take two for an answer.

He said, "You must eat three as God ordained."

"Who says God ordained three?"

"It is an old Russian hand-me-down," he said in English, "a man must always eat three eggs for breakfast—if he has them."

The young *provodnik* had bought us a newspaper at Kirov. The leading editorial concerned "summer holidays for school children" and stressed the importance of improving little minds and bodies at the same time. The chief foreign news article was a lengthy discussion of the German problem facing the foreign ministers in Paris.

Truth, Does It Matter?

The next day was bright, hot, dry. At a small station I photographed peasant women selling their produce and then the travelers on the top of the train. An unshaven air force captain, his collar open and his hair tousled, came up to me and said, in English: "Why do you take such pictures? What for? All times since we leave Vladivostok you make pictures these peasants."

"I am a correspondent. I am trying to document the trip."

"Why do you make these peasant pictures, please?" he insisted. He wore five big round red and gold enamel and metal medals on his tunic.

"I like their faces. We rarely see pictures of Russian peasants in America."

"Why do not you take Red Army men pictures?"

A crowd had formed a circle around us. I told the captain that I had made pictures of Red Army men.

"Do you speak French?" he asked.

"Badly."

"Oh, well. Why do you make picture about those men on train top?"

"Why not? It is interesting."

"It is *not* interesting. It is very bad. That picture will appear in England, will it not? Or America? That is very bad for our country."

"It's the truth, isn't it?"

"It does not matter truth or not. Take other pictures, please. Red Army men. Trees. Parks. You take pictures like that on train top all times since Vladivostok. I do not understand why it is so necessary for you."

"Because I am trying to show what this trip is like. Do you think it will do your country harm to have people elsewhere know that there is not enough transportation for all who want to travel? Naturally the reason must be explained, too. Americans understand thousands of cars were lost during the war. If you give the reasons for overcrowding, what harm is there in the picture? Do you want foreigners to believe that

133

Russia is perfect, that you have plenty of trains? Then when people come here they will be disillusioned."

The captain had his mouth open as if he were catching flies. "You spoke too fast," he said. "Will you say it later in French? My wife is French teacher in Moscow school. She wants to meet you. Have you ever been in France?"

"Yes, but it's been a long time."

"She teaches French but she has never spoken to anyone who has been in France. Will you speak to her? When?"

"Right now."

He pushed through the gathering. Presently he came back, dejectedly. "She cannot come now. She is washing her hair."

I walked away and took a few more pictures. Another soldier who had been listening, followed me. "Don't bother about that fellow," he said in Russian, "he just wanted to speak to an American. He just wanted to show he could speak American."

Lines in Praise

The restaurant director came around with a "praise and criticism" book and reminded Ageev that Moscow was only a day away. She would like it if Ageev and myself, her best and most regular customers, would please inscribe a few words about the service and the food. Ageev wrote several lines and handed the book to me.

"Should I sign in English or Russian?"

"In English. To them it will look more important."

Later a letter instigated by someone in the car, probably the *provodniks*, came around for signatures. It stated that the

provodniks had worked hard and well and that the under-
signed were satisfied.

The old man waited while we scribbled our signatures.
"Moskva! Moskva! Moskva!" he sighed. "Why do I love her so
after all these many years? For you young men it means
pleasure, for me only more work. I must count and change
all the linen, polish every centimeter of brass, especially the
spittoons, clean everything, everywhere."

"Keep it up," I told him, "you'll be a Hero of Socialist
Labor before you're seventy."

"Thank you, thank you. Don't forget, never travel on the
Trans-Siberian unless you sleep in wagon 2021. That's this
one." He saluted and left to take the letter of commendation
to the next compartment.

After four games of Russian dominoes I slunk away in dis-
grace to talk to the inhabitants of the space between cars.
Ageev had been my partner against Victor Ivanovich and a
merchant marine captain. They licked us easily in three
games, almost entirely due to my stupid blunders. One game
we won by a fluke: my blunders confused our opponents completely.

Dmitri and Igor: Veterans

When the girl from Birobidzhan left at Krasnoyarsk, my
favorite vestibule companion became a young flier, Dmitri
Kusanov, from Stalinagorsk, a town "under Moscow." After
six years in the army he was going home to be married to a
prewar sweetheart named Antonia. He showed me her picture. She had long pigtails, large breasts and a wide grin.

135

"She's lovely," I said.

Dmitri grinned happily. His dirty-blond hair was close cropped, his features were big and his face was friendly. He was wearing an oil-stained coverall. "It will be useful," he said, "I can make it into a smock." I resorted to the dictionary for "smock," did not find it, and finally had to have one of my navy friends translate for me. Even so, it is not an exact translation. There is a special Russian word for the garb which a painter wears. And Dmitri was a painter.

On this next to the last day he had been joined up front by a red-necked, runt-sized, bass-voiced officer without epaulets. His name was Igor Pavlovich Muriev and he had been a captain. Igor liked to talk.

He was seventeen and in his first year at the Institute in Kirov, when the war broke out. "I served on the Third Byelorussian front," he said. And then he let loose with a string of the names of German towns through which he had marched beginning with Koenigsberg and ending with Stuttgart. He sounded just like a train caller. "At Koenigsberg I was wounded. Shot through the head. I had three operations to save my eye."

His left eye had a strange cast, but I couldn't tell whether he could see out of it or not. Later Dmitri told me that Igor's eye was artificial. Or rather, it was an eye that had been made with a dead man's cornea.

"In May 1945," Igor boomed, "I was sent out to the Baikal front. That's when we had the Germans licked. I went out on this railroad."

Igor was twenty-two, born in a small town near Kirov.

His parents were farmers. "Now I am going to Moscow. To Moscow to study history and geography so I can go home and become a teacher." Igor said he had been in Poland, Czechoslovakia, Rumania, Bulgaria, and Yugoslavia. "Life in Czechoslavokia is better than anywhere else. Better than in the Soviet Union except for Moscow. What avenues! What homes! What schools! What lovely factories! And what's more, what a real appreciation they have of Russian culture as well as their own. Russian music in Prague—Tschaikowsky, Glinka, Borodin, Moussourgsky. And the Soviet composers are not forgotten, I assure you. Shostakovich, Prokofiev, Gliere, Khachaturian."

Dmitri wanted to know who was running the Czech government.

"Didn't you read the paper?" Igor was amazed. "The election is completed. The Communist party is now the first party. A Communist, I forget his name, is premier. Mister Beneš remains the president."

"A fine man," I said, "I've met him on several occasions."

"Well," said Igor, "I think I will climb into the other car. I think I have a chess game there. Excuse me." He let himself out the door, swung from the steps of our car to the next one and climbed in.

"This has been a hard trip for you, Dmitri."

"I do not want you to think that I must ride like this," Dmitri said. "I was a senior lieutenant in the air force. Here," he pulled something out of his coverall pocket, "you see I have a first class ticket and an order for a 'soft' berth. But I had no priority. It was necessary to wait for one week, maybe two weeks for a place. I am in a hurry, so I am standing here."

Suddenly little Igor came bouncing back. "No chess game for five minutes," he said in his deep bass, "and I want to ask our American companion one question. It is this. Do you think the war is over?"

"Yes, certainly."

Igor laughed harshly. "You are at best fifty percent correct. The military war is over, but the political war goes on. Look at China. Germany. Korea. Poland. Greece. Indonesia. France. Anywhere. The Czechs are all right. So are the Yugoslavs. And, of course, we Russians. But everywhere else, political war. Civil war in certain countries. Is that right?"

He didn't wait for my answer. He swung out the door again.

Dmitri said, "They fixed his eye but I am not so sure about his head. Do you think he talks a little strangely?"

"No. He is probably suffering from shock. But his ideas are sane enough."

Dmitri looked at his wrist watch which was as big as a Mexican dollar. "Fourteen more hours to Moscow. Think! Only fourteen more hours. Do you like to dance? I know them all—foxtrot, waltz, polka, mazurka. And pretty girls! And the ballet! And the theaters! And concerts, good concerts! and films! Maybe American films! I will stay in Moscow as long as my money lasts." He took a hefty wad of 100-ruble notes out of his pocket.

"Have you been robbing a bank?"

"No, that is my back pay for many, many months."

"Dmitri, seriously, what country won the war against Japan?"

"We did," he said, promptly.

"What about the United States and Great Britain and China?"

He frowned. "I am sorry," he said. "I forgot for the moment. Yes, of course, we all did. I did not mean the Soviet Union alone. I thought about Manchuria."

"Do most Russian soldiers understand that America fought against Japan for almost four years before Russia entered the Pacific war?"

"Oh, yes," he said, but he didn't sound certain. "We have read much about your bombing raids and about naval action on all the islands. But *we* really came into contact with the main part of the Japanese army." He paused. "That is right, is it not?"

I made an attempt to summarize the various phases of the war against Japan. When I had finished, Dmitri said: "If all that you have spoken is truth, I have not understood completely perhaps. But let me ask you, how many Americans or Englishmen understand completely the role of the Russian people in the war against Hitlerite Germany?"

"Many of them do. Perhaps not completely. It's difficult for people three thousand or more miles away to understand completely. I think too many of us have already forgotten what your country suffered in loss of men, homes, industry and resources."

"I am glad you are honest. I would like to go to America

139

with Antonia. Only to visit. Is there more to see and do in New York than in Moscow?"

To any Russian born in a small town or a small village, it is almost inconceivable that any place could be more glamorous, more modern, more wonderful, more amazing than Moscow. When you tell them about New York they listen politely, but inside they are sure you are bragging, that you are trying to run down Moscow. An Illinois dirt farmer might feel the same way about Chicago if he had never seen any other big city. Moscow, however, is more than a big city: it is the capital of all the Soviet Republics, the capital of Communism, the capital of the Russian Orthodox Church, the capital of Russian culture. It is metropolis and Mecca rolled into one.

Death on the Roof

About six in the evening just outside of Galich, a pleasant valley town on the Ozura River, I was sitting near the window when I heard a horrible scream, a thud above me and then a series of shrieks. Then someone pounded on the roof and yelled to stop the train. The young porter pushed through the car, yanked down an emergency lever which signaled the engineer. The brakes went on suddenly, I rocked forward. The young porter rushed out and I followed. A bloody body was dangling from the roof. The *provodnik* climbed onto the roof of the car and then descended, bearing in his strong arms the mangled remains of a young boy. Gently he laid him out on the ground between our train and the other set of tracks.

Passengers flocked out of the train. Everyone asked questions at once. The boy had been looking the wrong way when the train went under a low bridge. He had been hit in the back of the neck, knocked the full length of the car, killed almost instantly.

A doctor was summoned. She came, knelt down, sniffled, stood up and said what we all knew.

The train whistle kept shrilling. We all stood stock-still around the corpse. The whistle shrilled again and again. Still none of us budged. Then we heard the preliminary lurch as the train began moving. We ran for the steps, all of us except the young porter. He wheeled, raced into the bordering field, scooped up a fistful of weeds and wildflowers, rushed back, placed them on the boy's bare, red chest, and then caught up with the train.

At the next stop the car was washed with hoses. Passengers, now cautiously reclining, still rode on the top of the train. But not atop our car.

On the platform I met one of the new Soviet citizens whose name I never did discover. He was a heavy-set, middle-aged man with a fine set of store teeth. Previously, we had exchanged only perfunctory greetings.

"What's your impression of Russia now?" I asked him.

He accepted a cigarette, smiled and replied in English. "Everyone looks very healthy, very healthy. They seem to have enough food, don't you think so? I am surprised at large amounts of eggs, butter, *smetana* and meat for sale and how cheap it is. Of course, clothing and particularly shoes. . . ."

141

he shrugged. "But little children. How healthy they are after Chinese!"

"What did you do in China?"

The big man stared at me. "I am Diesel engineer."

"Where did you work? Shanghai?"

"Diesel engineer in China cannot make living as Diesel engineer. I am trader, store-keeper, mechanic, translator. I go there to help train Chinese engineers. I give it up. I need to eat. Finally I am so sick of whole business that I re-apply for my Soviet papers. They not only give me my papers, they also arrange for good job in Leningrad."

"You won't find life in Russia very easy either."

"I know it is not easy. That is why I leave years ago. To find easy life. There is no easy life today. But in Leningrad I am home and I will eat as much as other fellows. That is all I ask. I may even find one wife. Do you think I am too old?"

Message for Americans

Nobody in the car slept much that last night. Hidden stores of vodka and gin appeared from packing cases. The mounting excitement which always develops at the end of a long journey bubbled around the exploding point.

Victor Ivanovich fussed with Ageev's packing cases. Ageev, the colonel of engineers and the merchant marine captain persuaded him to relax for a while and sing. Victor Ivanovich had an excellent tenor voice. Over and over again he led them in singing "My Moscow." He insisted that I learn the chorus in Russian:

"Kipouchaya,
Mogouchaya,
Nikem nege pobedimaya,
Strana maya,
Moskva maya,
Tui samaya loubeemaya!"

Translated this boils down to: "Melting pot, unconquerable, my country, my Moscow, you are the most beloved!"

Some hours later we finished singing and drinking and we dozed off with our clothes on. At 5 A.M. the old *provodnik* made the rounds, pounding on doors, crying: *"Moskva skoro, Moskva skoro* (Moscow soon)," although the train was not due to arrive until ten. He repeated this Paul Revere act in a half hour and then every fifteen minutes until the entire car was roused and dressed.

At 6 A.M., about seventy-five miles from Moscow, the train stopped at Alexandrov and an electric engine replaced the locomotive. Ageev, Victor Ivanovich and I prepared an elaborate feast for our final breakfast. When it was over, I said to them: "For twelve days I have not asked you many questions about your feelings and your opinions. Now, before we part, I would like to ask your advice about one thing."

"O.K.," Ageev said. Victor Ivanovich nodded.

"I ask you this as my friends, not because you, Michael, are a Soviet government representative. I want your *personal* feeling as Soviet citizens. What do you think is the most important single thing for Americans to know about your country? What single fact will help them understand you?"

There was a long silence. Finally Ageev spoke. "As a correspondent you must ask that question of our top leaders.

143

You must ask Generalissimo Stalin or Foreign Minister Molotov." Victor Ivanovich heartily backed him up.

"I don't want their opinion now. I want to know what you and Victor Ivanovich think as Soviet citizens. I don't want you to tell me what you think *their* opinions would be either. I want yours. This is nothing official."

Ageev grasped it. He pondered, alternately chewing on his lower lip and fingering his moustache. "All right," he said finally. "Americans say Russia is spreading Communism in China. This is not truth. Americans must know this and understand."

I wrote down what he had said and turned to Victor Ivanovich. He was gazing abstractedly out of the window. "What about you?" I asked.

He was startled. "Me? I am a worker. An electrician by trade. I cannot decide such things."

I argued with him. But he was stubborn and he steadfastly refused to answer the question.

At 8 A.M. the two porters paced up and down the corridor spitting water onto the dust-heavy carpeting. They would pause in front of every compartment and ask, "Are you packed? Are you ready? *Moskva skoro!*"

The villages and towns close to Moscow had an air of permanence which made them differ from their counterparts in Siberia. The forests were no longer virgin, great sections having been chopped down. New wooden houses and barns were everywhere to be seen and new fences, too. The skyline changed. Each town had a recognizable old church turret.

At Zagorsk there were several of the familiar onion-bulb towers. During the last hour and a half we sped through dozens of suburban stations packed with patient people waiting for their commuters' trains. It might have been Westchester but not one was reading the *Herald Tribune*.

I left the window to say goodbye to a few of the passengers in the car. Zamenchek, the inspector of mines, asked me where I would be staying. "You asked me questions about our new housing program. I will try to find out for you and I will telephone you." We shook hands.

I couldn't locate Julie or Vassily. The general was standing in the corridor putting his uniform on over his Japanese pajamas.

The young flier, Dmitri, had gone into the bathroom and had changed into a clean uniform. "Can I show you Moscow or do you have friends there?" I wrote out my address and said I hoped he would get in touch with me. I sent my love to Antonia and also a small coral and silver pin I had bought in Peking. "Give this to her from an American. It's a wedding present." Dmitri stared at the pin for a moment. I had the feeling he would refuse it. But he didn't. Instead he threw his arms around me and squeezed me. When he released me he took the pin. "It is really much too beautiful," he said.

"Not too beautiful for Antonia."

"Not for Antonia." He grinned.

I gave the *provodniks* a half dozen cans of food, a bottle of sherry, cigarettes and a tip. They thanked me and before I was out of earshot the old man turned to the young one and said, "You understand now? I told you *all* Americans were gentlemen."

Noses were pressed against the windows as we reached Moscow. The last ten minutes seemed like ten hours. At last we pulled into the station. I could hear a collective sigh.

Ageev was met by a delegation from the Ministry of Foreign Trade. He shook hands and gave me his telephone number. "We will drink together again. Maybe you can learn how, you are young yet." He thanked me for my companionship.

Victor Ivanovich helped me to get my bags down. He was the last person I shook hands with. The last thing he said was: "About your question. I have been thinking very hard. As a Russian worker I have to tell you this: the most important fact for Americans to know about Russian people is that we want to live in peace."

The clock on the platform, as I stepped off, told me that the Trans-Siberian Express had not arrived in Moscow on schedule. We were three minutes early.

PART IV

THE WEARY ARE WARY
Moscow

THE last time I had been in Moscow was September 1944 when victory was so near yet so far; when every last ounce of material, every sagging bit of spirit was being squeezed into the final avalanche that swept the Russians to Berlin. Returning in June 1946, a little more than a year after the war's conclusion in the west, I found Moscow had changed. Superficially, at least, Moscow was brighter.

Spiraling up over the ancient walls of the Kremlin, the onion bulbs were being gold-leafed. Over the biggest department store a brand-new neon sign reddened the sky with Stalin's profile and an appropriate patriotic slogan. The pre-Revolutionary Metropole Hotel, where I was lucky enough to get a room, had been partially repainted for the first time in six or seven years. Its bar was still closed but a public commercial restaurant, as gaudy as a redecorated *Childs*, had opened on the ground floor. Moscow University had a fresh coat of canary-colored paint. The vestigial traces of camou-

147

flage were wearing off government buildings. A swanky ice cream parlor with shiny metal appointments and a "cocktail lounge" with silk curtains adorned Gorky Street (Moscow's Fifth Avenue). On this high-toned thoroughfare jeeps were not allowed; "not cultured," said the cops.

There was a new nightclub, the *Aurora*, with a *dzhaz band*. Merchandising displays in store windows were definitely snappier, although there was still no need for artistic talent to help sell their limited stocks. However, one of the fancier ladies' dress emporiums had staged a "fashion show with live models" for the Moscow housewife; the dresses were rather nice. The quantity of goods for sale had increased, the quality was still not prewar—and where is it?—but prices were down.

Little incidents in day-to-day living underscored the postwar changes. During the war, correspondents never quit their tables in the hotel dining room until they had gathered up every scrap of leftover bread. This helped to feed secretaries, couriers and chauffeurs. Now nobody bothers. Bread, while not over-plentiful, is no longer on Moscow's scarcity list. (Elsewhere in Russia it still is.)

In the same dining room the waiters had preferred a tip of two or three American cigarettes to ten or fifteen per cent of the check in rubles. Now that money can actually purchase many commodities in the stores, the waiters would rather receive rubles than cigarettes.

On my way to the Soviet Foreign Office to call on the Press Department I paused to buy an "Eskimo Pie." The price, which was forty rubles in 1944, had melted down to six. At the downstairs entrance to the Foreign Office I was stopped by a guard, as before. But this time when I explained my business he merely said, "Second floor." He had not bothered to telephone upstairs to check, nor had he asked me to show a *propusk* or passport.

Strolling back to the hotel I was struck by the greatly increased and variegated amount of traffic. Moscow was full of liberated automobiles, all sizes, models and makes—German, Polish, Hungarian, Czech and even a few Italian "Fiats." There were more busses, too, and some of them were new. The biggest shock was spotting a fairly empty bus. Moscow's transportation system was still overburdened, but the perennial lines of waiting workers at street corners were certainly shorter.

One day I revisited the Mostorg, the city's largest department store, and ran into a series of surprises. Firstly, there were factory-fresh radios for sale. During the war the government had confiscated all private sets; now old ones had been returned and new ones could be bought.

I asked a salesgirl the cost of the smart, silver-gray table models named *Rodina* (Motherland).

She said, "Six tubes, two thousand two hundred rubles."

"Can you hear foreign stations?"

"I think so."

"Can I buy one? Can anyone buy one? Do you need a special permit?"

The clerk smiled. "All you need is two thousand two hundred rubles."

There were also portable typewriters (four thousand rubles), sewing machines (two thousand two hundred rubles), gramophones (two thousand) and the Praktiflex, a low-priced German-made camera. More than a few of the stores' recently introduced items were of Central European origin.

I paused near an eye-catching array of gay red, blue and green plastic raincoats for women. They were priced at five hundred rubles. A salesgirl assured a dubious customer, "They are very good. German, you know. And German colors are very good. They do not run."

Cameras, sewing machines and plastic raincoats are the kinds of things Muscovites dreamed about at night during the long, weary war years. But during the day they were concerned with more pedestrian desires: shoes. Except for the blackest and most high-priced markets, civilian shoes could not be begged, borrowed or bought in Moscow for several years. The Red Army's requirements came first. In the spring of 1944 a small supply was released for sale on the third floor of the Mostorg. Only civilians with a specific ration card could buy them, and they had to enter the store through a special side entrance. In the mornings that first spring when I looked out of my Metropole window I saw hundreds of patient people shifting their poorly shod feet, waiting for the store to open. They brought along camp chairs, thermos bottles and parcels of food, prepared to hold the line as determinedly as baseball fans before the first world series game.

This, too, had changed. No special entrance, no long queue. In 1944 a shoeless Muscovite had to count out six to eight thousand rubles for footwear, black market, or four to five thousand at the Mostorg. Now fairly sturdy, not very stylish shoes are available at the Mostorg for five and six hundred rubles—a reduction of more than eighty per cent in price.

This does not mean that Moscow or the Soviet Union have enough shoes. They have not, most definitely. But the situation in Moscow is better and perhaps, in time, they will even have sufficient shoes to distribute in far-off villages like Zilovno.

Even the Slogans Are Tired

The people in Moscow had changed, too. The terrible pressure of the war was over and they were allowing themselves the luxury of being weary. Actually, it was more than weariness. Exhaustion is the better word. They had more food, a little more clothing; but, and understandably, they had less drive.

Anyone who has been working too hard night and day and seven days a week for four or five years needs a long rest. Ideally, when Stalin stood up in the Bolshoi Theatre on February 6, 1946, he should have announced a breathing spell, vacation, instead of another Five Year Plan. Unfortunately, Stalin had no choice. Russia's economy could not afford a breathing spell if its people were to continue to eat.

The few Russians in Moscow who trust me enough to talk freely were depressed—not by the Soviet attitude but by the American. Again in conversations the atom, the Churchill speech, the death of Roosevelt cropped up: three landmarks on the downhill path into the wilderness of American-Anglo-Soviet distrust and dissension.

I had one all-night bull-session with a Russian intellectual who, although not a party member, is a loyal Soviet citizen. This, as nearly as I can remember it, was what he said: "There is a crisis in the Soviet Union. Not a crisis of economics, you will have that I think. Ours is chiefly a crisis of the spirit. There is great evidence that the well springs of creative energy which every social earthquake releases are dangerously close to drying up. Perhaps they were drained too much by the war. Burned up, you say.

"My friend, we have a great weariness. Where does this lead us? The clinging after the past—in art, theatre, music, religion—is deep-rooted, after all. Once having been revived by them (the Politburo, understood) as a wartime measure, it could only be checked or reversed by a major campaign of propaganda.

"We are so weary. The slogans are weary. The words seem to have lost their life. Even the new banners look old and tired. But the people want something new. What excites them most in *Pravda*? A picture of the new low-priced car, *Pobeda* (Victory).

"The movies are very full. The nightclubs? You cannot get near the door unless you are somebody special. You must have noticed this weariness was with us during the war, but we kept going on nervous energy. We had the drive of the unifying force, the desire to survive and then to win. Victory, for a while, helped keep us going. Momentum. But now it has worn off.

"We have the new Five Year Plan, but it is really the old Five Year Plan with new dates and new goals. We want to see it fulfilled and it will be. But have you ever as a child worked very hard to build a castle in the sand and then have someone knock it over? You may rebuild, but the same esprit is not there. I know this is not child's play. We must push ourselves. But how to do it? At times like this, my friend, I am glad that I am not a party member. They must find a way."

At this point I asked him if he thought the current anti-American campaign might not be the way: to drive home the possibility of an attack on the Soviet Union by the capitalist nations and thus rally the people. He did not think so.

I had one other long and serious conversation with a Russian in Moscow which is worth reporting. This was with an older man, a scientist and a member of the party who, paradoxically, is humorous as well as doctrinaire. I questioned him about the weariness, about the possible solution, about Russia's foreign policy. He was very cautious in his reply.

"That there is this weariness of which you speak is true," he said. "But I still think we have more reserve strength. Russia needs her people to rise to new heights now as never before. And we will do it. You did not believe we could beat the Germans. We did. We will fulfill the plan. Our only fear is America. Not the American people but the American reactionaries who lead your people. If our press did not continually point out the dangers of an anti-Soviet coalition it would be failing in its duty to the state."

"If Russia had the atom bomb," I asked, "do you think now would be a good time to attack these reactionaries?"

The scientist was shocked. "It is a basic concept of our thinking that wars are started by capitalist nations. When

Stalin says we want peace, he means it. How could we use an atom bomb—if we had one, and I do not think we do—on America without destroying millions of workers, farmers and intellectuals who want peace and who do not follow your reactionary voices? Senator Pepper might even become radioactive. No."

I reminded the scientist of certain aggressive characteristics in Soviet policy which the western powers considered war-like. I cited their reluctance to withdraw troops from Iran according to the Teheran agreement. "On the same basis, might not the Soviet Union use force to gain her own ends elsewhere—providing she had that much force?" I asked.

"You should read Lenin and Marx and less of Walter Lippmann. (Lippmann had recently been a continual target of Moscow newspaper commentators)," the scientist said. "There are so many basic conflicts inherent in the capitalist system that the ultimate victory of socialism is assured. Why risk an atomic war? We Marxists believe that the wheel of history is turning in our direction. Look at the map of reaction and progress in 1914 and again in 1944 and then in 1946. Tremendous gains for Marxism. Of course, you have a point about Iran. Sometimes the wheel moves too slowly and we are tempted to give it a little push."

"What happens next in American-Russian relations?"

"The only prediction worth making is a certainty. The answer to what happens will be found in the next American presidential election, I think."

"If you were an American and could vote, whom would you support?"

"Mr. Roosevelt," he said quickly.

I said the obvious thing. "He's dead."

The scientist sighed. "You must not let him be dead. Lenin still lives with us."

An astute young Allied diplomat who has been stationed in Moscow since 1944 and who is a confidante of Byrnes and Bevin, although not always agreeing with them, also felt that the Russians had the reserve power and the will power to move ahead despite the evident national weariness. His views on why the Soviet press concentrated its fire against the United States were arrived at from a radically different viewpoint. "For a Russian Marxist," he pointed out, "the United States is now the main enemy because despite its defunct, strike-ridden system it is managing to give the coal miner and the shop girl more tinned goods, more dresses and shoes than any other country. To do just that—to raise the workers' living standard—is the aim of socialism. And so the main barrier to Russia's ideological progress in the world is the United States—or rather its standard of living; she tries to keep knowledge of that standard from her own people.

"In ten or fifteen years the Russians—they're good, mind you—can attain a higher standard than anywhere in the Far East, the Balkans, Europe, or even England. But not the United States. Technologically the United States is generations ahead of them. And so their press must try to show that life is not really so good in the United States, that there are strikes, unemployment, anti-labor legislation, discrimination against Negroes and so on." He paused and then added parenthetically, "You know, even if we gave them the atom bomb, the Russians cannot be certain we would not invent something else."

Without mentioning the scientist's name, I tried his line of reasoning on the diplomat. If the Politburo was sure of the ultimate victory of socialism, why carry a chip-on-the-shoulder attitude into every conference?

"I suppose they are sure," said the diplomat, "but not so sure as they would like to be. The Marxists predicted a clash between England and America before the last war— capitalist rivalry and that sort of thing, you know. It didn't come off. And it won't this time, either."

"Do you think Russia wants war?"

"Lord no! They carry that chip because they are afraid that appeasing us will give them a black eye at home and in the satellite states. We might take it as a sign of weakness and ask for more and more and more concessions. We could, too, you know. They are weak in a military sense and strong in that they have public opinion solidly behind them, while in England and America there are at least two sides to the great argument."

Why Correspondents Curdle

Most of the people I talked with in Moscow were other correspondents. The year of peace has not appreciably changed their lives, professionally. The average British or American correspondent in Moscow is still a man largely without contacts, sources or friends except his wife, his secretary, his file of Soviet newspapers and encyclopedias, his embassy and his fellow newsmen. There are, of course, exceptions and exceptional correspondents.

The average correspondent's housing situation is a trifle better. If he has not already acquired an apartment, he at least has been permitted to emerge from his cocoon sufficiently to have a separate hotel room for working and living. Censorship, which has supposedly undergone a change for the better, still frustrates him beyond words. Cables are no longer red-penciled by uniformed minions of the Press Department in the Foreign Office. Couriers may now carry copy directly to the Central Telegraph Office on Gorky Street instead of the Foreign Office. At the Telegraph Office the cables are perused by unknown, unseen censors who work for *Glavlit*, the chief Soviet literary board of review.

At first under this simplified arrangement there was a brief, black period when correspondents never found out the fate of their copy once it had been handed in; no reports were made; all attempts to talk to censors were rebuffed. This "blind" censorship is now over, theoretically. The unseen men of *Glavlit* are supposed to telephone and inform correspondents about deletions. Often they do not. In the period between May 1 and May 15, 1946, one correspondent discovered that a thousand words had not been transmitted and that these deletions had not been reported to him by the censors. He figured this out by comparing the word total he submitted and the word total on his bill for cable charges.

This streamlined method of censorship adds one more frustration to the reporters' unhappy life in Moscow. He no longer has the safety valve of being able to blow off steam in front of a censor's immobile face.

It is no wonder that the average correspondent turns bitter. Usually nothing is done to make his personal life easier or his work more productive.

Many correspondents never leave Moscow on a story although no one in his right mind would think of covering the United States only from Washington. When a trip is arranged for him, either he or his office are likely to dismiss it as "something they want us to see." When a trip isn't arranged, it's because of "something they don't want us to see." Laziness and fear also tend to keep the foreign correspondent in Moscow. Fear that while he is away something will "break" in Moscow—Stalin's death or the arrival of some world-famous potentate.

Yet when he stays in Moscow and keeps on top of the news, he is continually scooped by the Moscow Radio, which broadcasts news before it is released or before it is printed in *Pravda*. The Moscow wave lengths are monitored in London and rushed into print from there, often many hours before the Moscow correspondent even hears about the story.

During the war the competition was torrid among journalists to be the first to read, translate, rewrite and file the battlefront news from the Moscow morning papers. Now the bitter, bored correspondent and his equally bored Russian secretary spend their mornings in a search—not for Soviet breakthroughs against the Nazis—but for a fresh Soviet "attack" on the western powers.

One correspondent meeting another in the dining room (after he has filed his story) is likely to say: "I'll bet you didn't see that whopper in *Komsomolskaya Pravda* today which claimed that American school children are taught nothing but lies in their scientific books?"

This tidbit will give the other correspondent indigestion and send him back to his room and his newspapers to hunt up the slur on scientific education in the United States.

When the average correspondent finds it tough to make friends among the Russian people and officials (partly because editorials in his paper back home are lashing at Soviet policies), when his pet stories are killed, his frustration increases and there is little left but anger and perhaps a desire for retaliation. During the war in Chungking the average correspondent became just as furious with the restrictive measures and stupid methods of the Chinese Nationalist government; but there he could always gaze out across the fields at greener pastures. If he didn't like the Kuomintang, perhaps the Communists or the Democratic League would be more understanding. But in Moscow when he becomes angry and bitter the only greener fields are those at home. He begins to lose his objectivity about home and home policy; compared to the Russians, the politicians and policy-makers at home are one hundred per cent perfect.

The process of going sour is not fun. I have seen it happen to honest and competent journalists. I have felt my own system beginning to curdle on more than one occasion. Morning after morning during my stay there was some bitter little pill for an American or a Briton to swallow in the

Soviet press. It tasted all the more bitter because the foreigner in Moscow sees the world with one eye through the Soviet press; he cannot compensate by seeing with the other eye that many newspapers in New York, for example, are just as venomous in their attitude toward Russia. If a Russian correspondent were cut off from home and read his foreign news day by day only in the Hearst-McCormick-Scripps-Howard press he would become rather bitter about America's handling of the Soviet Union.

In the Soviet press, American actions are "imperialist" and even "fascist." In the American press, Soviet moves are "obstructionist" or the results of "Red imperialism." The great blessing of the American press is that it is not all the same. It ranges from red to yellow in its journalistic spectrum. This the Russians cannot understand. They quote only reactionary or extreme left-wing newspapers. An incident during my stay in Moscow illustrates the effect of this.

Lillian Hellman's *Watch on the Rhine* has been translated and successfully produced on the Moscow stage. In the first act the grand old lady of the anti-Fascist, liberal Washington family reads *The Daily Worker*. When I met the director I told him I thought the detail in the play was pretty authentic except that the lady would probably have been reading the Washington *Post* or the New York *Times*. He was amazed. "But she is a fighting liberal," he said, "therefore she *must* read *The Daily Worker*."

For a few days in Moscow I sampled the daily diatribe diet, although I did not write any stories. The day of my arrival *Pravda* reported from Paris that according to "reliably informed local journalistic sources" the Anglo-Americans had sinister designs on Italian sovereignty and independence which the Soviet delegation was defending. The British in particular, said the *Pravda* dispatch, have insidious ambitions to transform Italy into a "great military base."

Is this true, the whole truth? The Russian readers, millons of them, believe it is.

In the same issue *Pravda* quoted Hanson Baldwin, military writer for the New York *Times*, because he had made a point which they thought worth repeating. During the war the Soviet press had dubbed Baldwin as "the admiral of the inkpool" because he had failed sufficiently to recognize the valor of Russian arms. But on this day, two years later, *Pravda* boosted him because he had pointed out the strategic importance of a United States base in Iceland to our global military picture. Inferentially, the Russian reader assumes from this and similar articles that the Soviets must maintain an aggressive foreign policy in the face of an Anglo-American bloc which was busily securing bases unto itself—even in neutral Iceland.

On my second day, which coincided with the anniversary of Hitler's attack on the Soviet Union, Russia's foremost historian, Eugene Tarle, wrote an extremely important article (see appendix) claiming that American "imperialists" were trying to impose a *pax americana* upon the world through threats of force just as the Romans established *pax romana* upon the ancient world which they conquered and enslaved. On this date many United States newspapers were

underscoring the idea that Russia was now trying to re-
make most of the world on the Soviet pattern.

On June 23rd Tass reported from Paris that the plan to
place Trieste under international rule of the United Nations
did not "justify Yugoslavia's national aspirations." It did
not mention Italy's national aspirations; the idea was that
England and the United States alone for selfish reasons
opposed giving Trieste to Tito. Another article viewed
with alarm the arrival of British and American warships in
Trieste.

"What would the New York newspapers write if Soviet
warships suddenly steamed into Trieste while the subject of
jurisdiction was still under discussion in Paris?" a Russian ac-
quaintance asked me.

"They'd splash it all over page one," I told her, "and the
State Department wouldn't be five minutes behind the British Foreign Office in sending Molotov a sharp note."

"The Trieste problem does not worry me so much," she
said. "My family and I are concerned about the dispatch from
Washington which you probably did not even notice. The
one that tells about your congressional appropriations for
permanent military bases in Alaska, the Marianas, the Phil-
ippines, Hawaii and Okinawa. Do you need those bases to
fight the Spaniards? Or the Australians?"

I said our Navy just liked real estate, but I could see why
she was worried.

About this time in world history Bernard Baruch made his
proposal on atomic control. For several days the fact went
unreported in the Soviet press. On June 24th *Pravda* re-

jected the Baruch plan without printing its text. The plan was turned down because, *Pravda* said, it consecrated the American monopoly of secret bombs; it would destroy the right of veto; it aimed to establish world domination by the powers with the atomic secret. "Why?" editorialized *Pravda*, "why are all other countries obliged to display blind confidences in the United States' intentions while the United States obviously distrusts not only its partners but also the international control organ (U. N.)?"

Although self-criticism is not permitted in the realm of Soviet external affairs, it is again being encouraged internally. On June 26th all the Moscow papers carried a long account of the Ministry of State Control's purging and committing to trial factory directors, engineers and accountants who have been faking production figures, receiving bonuses illegally, misappropriating factory funds for personal uses. This was the first time such sweeping charges had been publicly aired since the war's start; it opened the floodgates for subsequent criticism of industry, agriculture, trade unions, local Soviets, party functionaries, the theater and even literary magazines.

Reading the Moscow papers again over a period I was reminded of two important facts which many Americans fail to consider. First, everything in the Soviet press is written for home consumption; in China, for example, even news stories are slanted solely for foreign consumption. Correspondents then rewrite the stories and cable them. Practically nobody reads the press in China; one of the best Chinese newspapers has a circulation of about twenty thousand. *Pravda's* is over four million.

Second, the language of Soviet criticism is not dulcet. The sledge-hammer tactics, the name-calling, is all a part of Soviet critical journalism whether the man castigated is Russian film director Sergei Eisenstein or American correspondent Brooks Atkinson. There is no special brand of vitriol hoarded up for non-Russian "backsliders."

The Soviet press is almost never playful. *Crocodile*, the humorous weekly, tries its best and occasionally manages a sharp satire on Soviet inefficiency or bureaucracy. All its humor is functional. The week that the Ministry of State Control cracked down on the grafters, *Crocodile* reported the case of a twenty-five-year-old girl who was a food shop manager. She had stolen three hundred thirty-three thousand rubles. Arrested and tried, she was proven guilty. The sale of all her possessions brought the State only five thousand rubles. The girl manager was ordered by the court to repay the rest of the three hundred twenty-eight thousand at the rate of twenty-five per cent of her monthly wages. She was paid two hundred twenty-five rubles per month. The *Crocodile* report wound up with this directive to the embezzler: "There. You have your orders. You are directed to live until the age of 511 years."

A Soviet Editor's Opiate

The biggest local news of the week in Moscow was the session of the World Federation of Trade Unions' Executive Committee. This left-wing organization claimed to represent sixty-six million workers in fifty-six countries. One afternoon Solomon Lozovsky, acting for the absent Foreign Minis

ter Molotov, gave a reception for the delegates at Spiro-
donivka Palace. The next night at the *Dom Soyuzov*, the
building where the Trotsky trials were held, the delegates
gave the press a conference.

Sir Walter Citrine of Great Britain, the retiring president
of the WFTU, presided, sitting between Vassily Kuznetsov,
head of the Soviet trade unions, and the French delegate,
Louis Saillant, general secretary of the WFTU. I came in late.
Citrine was reading cut and dried announcements. The
WFTU had demanded that it be allowed to affiliate with the
United Nations and "to take part in the work of the United
Nations Economic and Social Council." It also called upon
the United Nations to recognize as "the legal constitutional
government of Spain" the Republican government-in-exile
of José Giral.

The foreign press knew that there had been hot debates
within the committee on the subject of Spain. Thus far during
the meeting the Soviet censors had refused to pass much
more than the official communiqués regarding the work of
the executive committee. American and British newspaper-
men made it plain to Sir Walter that they thought more lee-
way was desirable. Sir Walter was tart and firm in his negative
rejoinder to this request. Kuznetsov had already declared
that censorship was no concern of the WFTU. Citrine told
us that we must "abide by the local rules and regulations."

When the conference broke up, several of us paused to have
a bottle of beer in the anteroom. Michael Borodin, the man
who had been sent as the Third International's emissary to

help Sun Yat-sen organize the Chinese revolution in the early twenties, strolled over to say hello. For the past decade he has been editing the Moscow *Daily News.* Borodin, who now resembles nothing so much as a portly, conservatively dressed, successful business man, stroked his walrus moustaches and asked how we had liked the conference. Someone told him in no uncertain terms that it "stank" and offered him a beer. Borodin accepted.

"Well," he chuckled, "it's just lucky for you fellows that Citrine is not running this country instead of us. He'd be a lot less lenient with the press than we are."

"I'd be willing to take my chances," said Eric Downton, a Canadian who represented Reuters, the British news agency.

The talk then devolved around the frustrations under Soviet censorship and the limitations on foreign correspondents. Borodin said: "I am in a mood to tell you why we feel the way we do about you. It's a matter of philosophy. It's simply this: no newspaperman ever stopped a war but they've done a lot toward starting wars. We prefer to meet you like this—or at dinner or lunch or breakfast with vodka and caviar—rather than on a field of battle with guns and bayonets."

None of us had a ready answer and Borodin felt encouraged to continue. "You have to be philosophical about censorship," he said. "You must learn to understand our philosophy of the press." He went on making generalizations, referring to "philosophy" over and over again until Downton said: "I see what you mean. You want philosophy to be the opium of the press."

"Hah, that's a good one. I admit it," said Borodin. "Good night." He walked off.

Our Ambassador

One of the best contacts a correspondent has in Moscow is his country's ambassador. I called on the new United States Ambassador, Lieutenant General Walter B. Smith. General Eisenhower's former Chief of Staff is a slight, wiry man who looks you squarely in the eye, talks straight to the point and pulls very few punches. We discussed the situation in Japan and China, and I told him a little about my trip across Siberia. Then he talked about his job. Many of the things that he said were presumably off the record, although no formal warning was given.

As a good soldier Ambassador Smith is carrying out the State Department's orders to the best of his ability. He has no "Russian" policy of his own. The only thing I heard him say on the subject was that we must be "firm" with the Russians and not "tough." In a relatively short time the new envoy has learned a good deal about conditions in the Soviet Union. He is a man who knows how to use his staff wisely; in other words, I found him well briefed. He also has a certain amount of healthy humility. He understood the enormity of the problem (United States-Soviet relations) which he was tackling, and he had a sense of his own limitations and the limitations of his information. But he seemed to have great energy and the good old American trait of wanting to find things out for himself. In time he might become fenced in by diplomatic red tape in Moscow, but I don't think he is the type of man to stop giving his job everything he has. Whether he will ever understand the problem as well as he understands its enormity remains to be seen.

The Ambassador said he had been out paying a visit to Madame Kollantai, one of the "old Bolsheviks." The Soviet Union's envoy to Sweden during the war years, she is now engaged in writing her memoirs. The Ambassador had gone to her simply as a novice in the field of diplomacy to ask the advice of a veteran. "How do I get along with the Russians?" General Smith asked. Madame Kollantai told him that the Russians had no manners; he must learn to disregard that. As to advice, she could only counsel patience. "So if I meet a stone wall," said the General, "I am going back again and again and again and maybe they will change their attitude."

Although the Soviet newspapers were blasting the United States, and the American press was going to town against the Russians, the Ambassador was not overly pessimistic. He had a hunch, and probably more than a hunch, that agreements would and could be reached on most outstanding issues. The Soviet press and Foreign Minister Molotov had rejected "internationalization" for Trieste. "But," said Smith, "I think in the long run they will come around to that. It takes them time to change their stand." He was right.

Our discussion swung around to Soviet science and medicine. The Ambassador enthusiastically launched into an account of how he had personally gone out to talk to the Roskins, the man-wife biology team which had turned up a promising new cancer cure. When the Ambassador found out that I knew nothing about the cancer cure development, he began explaining it.

"KR" for Cancer

I was not making notes at the time and therefore cannot exactly retell the Ambassador's own version of what may become one of the most exciting personal scientific success stories since that of the Curies. But he stimulated my interest sufficiently so that I managed to obtain the details and check them in Moscow. I have added, parenthetically, figures on cancer in the United States which intensify the importance of the Soviet experiments.

In a badly ventilated laboratory at Moscow University two people are working on experiments which may someday save the lives of seventeen million Americans now living. One American dies of cancer every three minutes. During World War II the United States lost about two hundred and seventy-five thousand in action; in the same period of time almost five hundred thousand Americans succumbed to cancer. Another half-million Americans have cancer today and statistics gathered in the Surgeon-General's office in Washington indicates that one out of every eight persons living in the United States today will eventually die of cancer: seventeen million people.

While the United States Congress still has not approved a bill to have the government, which spent two billion dollars on atomic bombs, appropriate one hundred million dollars to combat cancer,* the Soviet government has spent many

* Private institutions in America invest heavily in the fight against cancer.

times that much in the past decade on experiments to find the cause and cure of the dread disease.

One of these hundreds of experiments is now beginning to offer a ray of hope. For over twenty years Professor Grigory Iosefovich Roskin has been devoting himself exclusively to cancer research at Moscow University. Roskin is a tall, gaunt man with an intent, ascetic face and piercing, deep-set blue eyes. Until 1937 he had consistently failed in his quest for something which would destroy the cells of cancerous growths and would not, at the same time, attack the normal, healthy cells surrounding the cancer. It was during 1937 that, by sheerest chance, he hit upon a piece of information which impelled him to take up a fresh approach to this problem.

In a Soviet medical journal he happened on a treatise about Chagas disease, a usually fatal infection indigenous to wide areas in South America. The article claimed that Chagas disease spread most rapidly in the breast of *female* victims. Since the female breast is also highly susceptible to cancer, Professor Roskin read on. By the time he had completed the reading of the treatise he was gripped with this idea: if the triatoma, the South American insect whose bite causes Chagas disease, preferred mammary cells, it was conceivable that it would also prefer cancer cells.

Impatiently Roskin waited for the importation of triatomas so that he could commence experimentation. When they arrived he locked himself into his laboratory and set to work. In one "control" jar he placed mice with implanted cancers. These he left alone. In another similar jar he placed another group of mice with implanted cancers. Into this second jar Roskin also introduced a few hungry triatomas.

The mice in the first jar died of cancer within a short period of time. The mice in the second jar with the triatomas continued to live and their cancers regressed. Elated, Roskin removed sections of the cancerous tissue from the mice in the second jar and eagerly examined them under his microscope. The cancerous tissue was half destroyed and contained active trypanosomes of Chagas disease, introduced by the bite of the triatoma.

Roskin felt that one point had been established. The trypanosomes of Chagas disease *did* prefer cancerous tissue to normal tissue. But when they were finished destroying the cancer cells they continued to devour the normal, healthy cells. There was not much point, Roskin reasoned, to check cancer at the cost of giving the patient Chagas disease, which also has a high rate of mortality.

During 1938 Roskin continued to ponder over this problem. He came to the conclusion that it was *not* the parasitical trypanosomes of Chagas disease which attacked and destroyed the cancer but an unidentified chemical secreted by the trypanosomes. This chemical he was unable to isolate. At this juncture he sought the advice and aid of his wife, Doctor Nina Georgievna Klyueva. An acknowledged expert in microbiology at Moscow University, small, dark-eyed Doctor Klyueva brought to her husband's experiments a theoretical and practical background in the preparation of serums and vaccines. She studied the history of her husband's experiments and then told him what was obviously the next step: "Since it is some unidentified substance within the trypanosome and not the living microorganism itself which destroys the cancer cells, why would not a dead trypanosome be as effective as a living one—and less lethal?"

Roskin saw the logic of this argument. At this critical moment, the war intervened. But Roskin and Klyueva went on working. They found that a solution made from the dead trypanosomes of Chagas disease attacked cancer but did not cause Chagas infection. Then the importation of further triatomas from South America became impractical, and their experiments were delayed several years. In 1943 the Soviet government arranged for a special shipment of the insects from Venezuela and the husband and wife resumed work.

Their immediate goal was the development of a solution from the dead trypanosomes which would be both stable and sterile and which could be standardized. This stage in their work was extremely frustrating; on several occasions they almost abandoned their search. Finally Doctor Klyueva developed a standard solution. The doctors christened it "KR" for their initials.

With "KR" they resumed laboratory tests with cancerous mice and with healthy mice. "KR" had a definitely beneficial effect upon the diseased animals, no effect on the healthy ones. The momentous question still remained: what effect would "KR" produce when injected into human beings?

Without a word to his wife, Professor Roskin made himself the guinea pig. He injected himself with "KR". For twelve tense days he went about his work trying to act as if nothing unusual had transpired. At regular intervals he cautiously checked his temperature, recorded his pulse and searched for unusual symptoms. There were no recognizable ill effects. Roskin felt as well as ever. He broke the news of the experiment to his wife who was, by turns, frightened, astonished and gratified.

Having hurdled this obstacle, Doctors Kyueva and Roskin decided they could make a preliminary report to the Soviet Academy of Science. This was done early in 1946. Their superiors were impressed by the body of evidence which the two doctors presented and urged them to continue.

The tests, however, are still far from conclusive, although "KR" is being used in the treatment of human beings suffering from cancer. Lack of serum has limited the scope of its application. In a dozen or more cases "KR" has reportedly reduced or partially destroyed cancers. Clinical reports showed that the new preparation has little effect on cancer of the skin, but was helpful in instances of cancer of the throat, of the cervix, of the uterus and of the breast.

One was the case of a middle-aged man with a throat cancer. Though small in size, the ulcer of the pharynx blocked the esophagus and was so situated that surgeons decided against an operation. Up to this point X-ray treatment had not been effective. Then the Roskins were called in. They began regular injections of "KR" (the quantity has not been revealed) while the X-ray treatment continued. By the fifteenth day the cancerous tissue was completely destroyed.

"KR" has at least two other drawbacks in addition to its

present limited supply. The most important is that at present strength the serum causes the disintegration of the cancer cells much more rapidly than healing tissues will grow to replace them. Therefore "KR" cannot be introduced in cases where the destruction of the cancerous tissue would result in the fatal malfunction of the body.

The second drawback is that the doctors have not yet found a satisfactory method for storing "KR". It must be used within a short period after its preparation or its effect does not necessarily remain constant.

"We do not claim this is *the* cancer cure," the Roskins insisted when Ambassador Smith called on them. "We require much more clinical evidence. But when we have learned how to store "KR" we promise that it will be shipped to the United States so that your doctors and scientists may share our experience."

Housing is a Headache

During my stay in Moscow I tried several times to reach Ageev, my traveling companion, at the Ministry of Foreign Trade. The last time I called the operator finally gave me his extension but he was out of Moscow visiting his wife. I never saw or heard from any of my Trans-Siberian train acquaintances except Zamenchek. He came while I was out and left a note with the clerk at the floor desk in the Metropole saying that such and such issues of *Izvestia*, *Red Star* and *Trud* carried good summary articles on the housing situation. He had wanted to set up an appointment for me with the Minister of Home and Civil Construction but that executive was "too busy." However, his office would give me any information I required.

On my first tour through the Soviet Union (1935) I had a special interest in the subject of housing and town planning. With few exceptions, I was disappointed in Soviet efforts at economical, functional building. Their architecture was eclectic, their workmanship far below our standards, and even their planning showed lack of taste and imagination.

Moscow, in particular, has always had a more severe housing problem than any other world capital. In 1935 it was not uncommon for three families to be bunched together in a small, badly ventilated two- or three-room apartment. At that time the housing shortage was a laughing matter which everyone expected to be straightened out by the end of the third Five Year Plan. The Soviet author Valentine Kataev wrote a play, *Squaring the Circle*, which poked some fun at enforced collective living.

Today, however, nobody laughs very loudly about collective living in Moscow. During the war years Moscow's population of three million, five hundred thousand nearly doubled. The housing situation deteriorated rapidly from bad to worse and it has produced chiseling on prices. As in other Soviet cities, rents are fixed by law. But landlords and tenants, with a capitalist hangover, have been demanding "key money" before they will surrender apartments or rooms to prospective customers. Quite a few have been caught and punished for taking bribes, and last summer all Moscow (especially the foreigners) was agog over the news of an axe murder committed as a result of the housing shortage.

Historically, housing has been one of the thorniest, unsolved problems for Soviet society. In the first and second Five Year Plans actual construction was fifty per cent below the official target. Things were progressing better under the third Five Year Plan; then the war set the planners back a couple of decades. All construction work, except on war plants, ceased. The Nazi armies during their invasion and retreat destroyed *six million* structures representing shelter for twenty-five million people. Incidentally, four million of the six million destroyed were privately owned dwellings.

These figures are so staggering that most Americans, concerned with their own housing shortage (and not a building bombed), cannot fully comprehend them.

The loss of six million homes? That is the equivalent of all the dwelling space at present in:

Alabama
Arizona
Arkansas
California
Colorado
Connecticut
Delaware
Florida
Georgia
Idaho
and the District of Columbia.

Housing for twenty-five million people destroyed? That's the same as saying that the United States had to find homes for all the inhabitants of these fifteen largest cities:

New York
Chicago
Detroit
Los Angeles
Baltimore
Cleveland
St. Louis
Boston
Pittsburgh
Washington
San Francisco
Milwaukee
Buffalo
New Orleans
and Minneapolis.

In addition to the homes destroyed, thousands upon thousands of buildings from Moscow to Vladivostok, untouched by the war, suffered from lack of proper maintenance and repairs.

The Soviets have always been so far behind in their building schedule that they have never had time to build carefully. Although they seldom confessed it to foreigners, Soviet insiders knew full well that the huge workers' apartments which mushroomed so rapidly in the late twenties and early thirties would never stand the wear and tear of even peacetime years. "We were inexperienced in such fundamentals of construction as mixing cement properly," a professor of architecture named Simonov confessed to me in 1944.

Now the Russians are setting about reconstruction, bedeviled by lack of men and materials. Skilled workers in the building trades are unbelievably scarce. This is one reason why the classified "want" advertisements for such workers appear in Soviet newspapers from coast to coast. It is also one reason why the Russians are so anxious to utilize German and Japanese labor for reconstruction.

Machinery of every description has to be spread thin over the Soviet Union. In building, first priority on men, machines and material goes not to housing but to factories and plants; second priority is for schools and hospitals; dwellings are a poor third. As a result of this allocation system, the limited available supply of excavators, ditch-diggers, bulldozers and cranes are employed in industrial construction, while most of the home-building, according to the Ministry of Home and Civil Construction, "is done by hand labor."

In the last phases of the war much was printed in Soviet periodicals about the wide postwar possibilities of prefabrication. Model houses were displayed in key cities; competitions were held for the best designs. But the experience of the past year has been disappointing. Prefabricated houses have been shoddily made. The Ministry of Home and Civil Construction has received reports from purchasers that "my porch fell to pieces the second day the house was up" and "the rain comes in the roof and through cracks in the window sills" and "the pipes for the oven do not draw properly."

Nor have the Russians been satisfied with the new "mansion" type house that postwar architects blueprinted for them. These small, privately owned one- and two-family bungalows looked pretty on paper. But due to over-quick production, inadequate machinery and technicians, these pretty-bungalows-on-paper are turning out to look like the crates-with-windows which I visited on Kalinin Street in Vladivostok.

Commenting on the results to date, the Soviet Union's Architectural Commission said pointedly: "The newly constructed residential districts and streets are uncomfortable, dull and ugly. In order to correct such defects we ought to use much greater means in future. Construction that is deceptively cheap is actually wasteful."

The new Five Year Plan set aside 42,000,000,000 rubles (about three billion, five hundred million dollars) to finance the construction of seventy-two million square meters of new housing; about a fifth of this amount will be spent in urban centers. This sum has already proven inadequate except for reconstruction of the ruined areas. In August 1946 another billion rubles was appropriated as a housing fund for workers in Siberia who were interested in constructing their own homes.

As of June 1, 1946, the Soviets had managed to put up 1,260,000 new rural homes since the war's end, accommodating about five million people. In the cities, almost three million citizens have been rehoused. Despite these great strides, seventeen million homeless human beings are still taking shelter in dugouts, boxcars, tents, hovels, caves, hallways, barracks, trenches, former restaurants and with their mothers-in-law.

On my arrival in Moscow I asked one of the American correspondents whether there had been many new buildings in the city since victory. He pointed up the street from the Metropole toward Lubyianka Prison.

"See that new wing on the jail?" he demanded. "Well, that's the only new construction since you left."

The correspondent, a rather cynical character, may have been joking. One afternoon I set out with my camera in a car driven by a husky young ex-Partisan named Leonid. Without leaving any of the main thoroughfares I saw many dozens of new buildings in Moscow's residential areas. Many of them were apartment houses which had been half or two-thirds completed on June 22, 1941. Now, five years later they were being completed or readied for occupancy.

While I was making this "housing" tour my camera inspired another amusing incident. I was standing on a Moscow River bridge photographing a very attractive housing development along the bank. A tall, angular woman, fairly well-dressed, approached me and said sternly: "What right have you to take pictures from a bridge?"

I started to answer when Leonid hopped out of the car, his face crimson with anger. Hands on his hips, he strode right up to my questioner.

"What right have you to interrogate this man?" Leonid demanded.

"The right of every Soviet citizen," responded the woman.

"I, too, am a Soviet citizen," Leonid said, "and I think it is fine that he is taking pictures of our Moscow."

"It is against regulations," the woman insisted. "He must stop."

"Let me see your credentials," Leonid suggested.

The woman glared at him.

"If you think it is against the law," Leonid said, "let us both go to the nearest police station and let them decide. Come on."

I was laughing. The bewildered woman took one frightened look at me, one at Leonid, and then fled as fast as her long legs would carry her.

PART V

MAJOR SOKOLOV SOUNDS OFF
Moscow to Berlin

SEVERAL hours after I was installed in my room at the
Metropole the telephone rang. It was Intourist demanding
to know how soon I was leaving Moscow. I told them in a
week or two. "But you must leave at once—tomorrow or the
day after," they said.

"Why? I was told that I could stay in the Soviet Union for
thirty days after the date of my arrival in Vladivostok. I have
more than two weeks remaining."

"That is correct. You may stay in the Soviet Union for
thirty days. But not in Moscow. You have a transit visa and
as we understand it you must stay *in transit* for thirty days."

If we hadn't been speaking English I would not have
believed my ears. But it was all perfectly serious. Intourist
wanted to put me on the next train for somewhere. I protested: "Your Ambassador in China said I could remain in
Moscow. He even said I could probably get an extension and
stay longer than thirty days."

Intourist was sorry. Their orders came from OVIR; OVIR represents the initials of the bureau which checks on visas.

I had been invited to spend the week at a *dacha* near Moscow with some Soviet intellectuals—writers, artists and composers whom I had met on my previous trip. Instead I had to remain behind to straighten out the matter of a special permit for staying in Moscow. The red tape on this would take many paragraphs to describe; I am saving those paragraphs for another visa problem. I wangled a letter from the Press Department of the Foreign Office which requested Intourist to request OVIR to allow me to stay another ten days in Moscow.

The real visa headache began when I tried to arrange my departure. I had explained to the Soviet Ambassador in China that I planned to leave Moscow by plane for Berlin and Paris. He had raised no objection. But when my passport was sent by Burobin (the organization which handles such matters) to the airlines office with the request for a plane passage to Berlin, it was refused. The courier returned: the point of exit from the Soviet Union in my visa was "Brest" (Brest-Litovsk.) There were no planes to Brest. I must take the train.

The overland trip through the Ukraine and Poland did not sound inviting after twelve long days and nights on the Trans-Siberian. I had wanted to reach Paris before the Council of Ministers meeting broke up. Frantically I telephoned Intourist, Burobin, the airlines, the Foreign Office, the American Embassy. No, if it was Brest on the visa it had to be Brest.

In desperation I called on the acting chief of the Press

Department and repeated my conversation with the Soviet Ambassador in China. The acting chief was very sympathetic.

"Your exit point should be Brest," he told me. "However, if you can get a passage by air for sure, we can see to it that you leave from Moscow."

I went back to the airlines office and told them my story. They were less sympathetic but also understanding. "Orders is orders," is about what they said. "If you get permission from the Foreign Office to leave with Moscow as your exit point, we will give you a ticket."

For a while I thought the merry-go-round would never cease. I returned to the Foreign Office. Couldn't they please change the visa to read *"Moskva"* instead of "Brest?" No, the issuing authority had been the Ambassador in China. To alter the visa was "very difficult." However, if I could secure a ticket they would. . . .

I let the matter ride for a few days. Then I sent a courier to the airlines office again. She was instructed to say, very firmly, that the Foreign Office had agreed to let me leave the Soviet Union at Moscow. At the same time I called the Foreign Office and told them I had secured a ticket by air.

I don't know whether or not they ever checked with each other, but I got my ticket. A few days later I reported at the airport, had my baggage weighed, paid for some excess, and boarded the plane. It was a twin-motored DC-3, built in the Soviet Union from Douglas plans.

To my amazement, there was no baggage inspection, no passport control. Passengers got on, filled all the seats. More passengers got on, filled the aisles. Everyone smoked. There were no safety belts. The plane was wheeled into position and without any warm-up took off and bumped a strong air current at 500 to 800 feet, the level at which most Soviet pilots prefer to fly.

An officer attached to the plane's crew shoved his way through the crowd and asked the men to rise and give their seats to the ladies who were standing. We all complied except one bull-necked colonel who said he had paid as much for his seat as everyone else (1,200 rubles) and he was not going to be penalized for being a male.

I was pushed up rather tightly against a stout officer who introduced himself as Major Sokolov. He kept his garrison cap on, and the peak seemed to be resting on his heavy, bushy eyebrows. He needed a shave. Sokolov inquired if I spoke German, and when I replied in the negative we proceeded to converse in English. Sokolov said that he was with the Soviet military government in Berlin, and I gathered that he may have been an intelligence officer. If so, he garnered nothing from me; he gave out with the intelligence.

Sokolov asked what I knew about the Soviet land reform program in the Russian zone of Germany. When he found out that I knew practically nothing, he gave me the works. "We will not make same errors that we made at first in Russia. This time we are providing land for workers and peasants—many settlers from Eastern Prussia, which is now Poland—and also establishing large-scale farms for mass production of grain and other much-needed foodstuffs." Then he rattled off the figures: how many acres to landless workers, how many to small farmers, to tenants, to new settlers and how many for "collective" farms. If the ride had been less bumpy I would have put them down. But it was difficult enough to stand without trying to take notes.

Koenigsberg Is Not Brest

After five nauseating hours we landed, not at Berlin but at Koenigsberg. This ruined city, the former seat of the *Junkers* in East Prussia, is now in Soviet territory and has been renamed Kaliningrad. Everyone left the plane, a green-hatted captain collected our passports, and two young girls commenced inspecting baggage. I waited impatiently for an hour. In my raincoat were rolls of film, undeveloped, uncensored. I had been more afraid of Soviet developing than Soviet censorship. If the films had been questioned I would have turned them over to the officials with the request that they be sent back to my Moscow office.

None of the passengers, except Sokolov, spoke to me. In fact they all regarded me with an air of suspicion—much more so than the passengers on the *Smolny* or on the train. Most of them were army men, some with their families. Perhaps it was because they saw Sokolov conversing with me that they remained discreetly silent.

I jotted down some notes on what Sokolov had said, and then I went up to one of the girl customs inspectors and asked her please to look at my baggage.

"What's your nationality?" she inquired.

"I am an American."

She smiled. "Oh, well. We will not look at your baggage at all."

Why or how this happened I do not know. There were tales in Moscow that the customs people were becoming increasingly strict. The men in Vladivostok had certainly been thorough. But nobody ever opened one of my bags on the way out of Russia.

We were all back in the plane. The green-hat had listed the numbers of our passports and visas. The door was closed. The propellers turned over. Then there was an insistent rapping on the door. The motors were turned off. The door was opened. The green hat asked, "Please, will the American be so kind as to come here?"

I jumped out. The green hat took my passport. "I beg your pardon," he said in Russian. "I have just seen that your exit point is Brest. This is Koenigsberg, not Brest." I said I knew that. "Well, then you understand," he said, forcing a smile, "you must return to Moscow on the next plane and go to Brest." He called to one of the crew to unload my baggage.

"Wait a minute," I said. "I'm not going back to Moscow. Isn't there someone here in authority whom I can talk with?"

The green hat bridled. "I am in authority."

I begged his pardon. Patiently I explained that the Foreign Office in Moscow had given me permission to leave by air without going to Brest.

"Please, I am glad," he said. "May I see that permission?"

"I have nothing in writing," I said.

"Then you do not have a *propusk*," he stated flatly.

"I do."

"You do not. Please produce it."

187

"One little minute," I said, trying to remain calm. "I am a foreigner. I received my ticket through Burobin. You have heard of Burobin? Good. Burobin is a good, responsible Soviet organization which works for foreigners. Do you think they would sell me this air ticket for Berlin if it had not been all right with the Foreign Office?"

"Please," he said. "Where is your ticket?"

I produced it. He inspected it carefully, noted down its number, and returned it to me. "Please, you may fly to Berlin, of course," he said. "I hope you will excuse me. I thought you *wanted* to go to Brest because your visa said Brest. This is Koenigsberg, not Brest."

We shook hands and I climbed back onto the plane for Berlin.

Germany: Point of Danger

For a half hour or more Sokolov did not speak to me; he replied to my occasional questions with grunts or nods. I did not feel much like conversation myself, but Sokolov seemed like too good a source to pass up. I asked him how the Russians were getting along with the Americans and British in Germany.

"With Americans—not good, not bad. Sometimes good, sometimes bad. With British—nearly always bad," he said.

"Why the difference?"

"Shall I tell you what I really think? I think it is because British have better discipline. Sometimes you Americans, as people, are fine for co-operation even if your government and your policy is anti-Soviet and anti-democratic. But when

British policy is that way, British officers—how is it you say
—toe the line. Is that right, toe the line? Well, every British
toe is on British line."

I resisted telling him he had made a bad pun.

"It's the old argument," I said. "You say *we* are anti-
democratic, we say *you* are anti-democratic."

"We? Never!"

"I don't believe it, Major. In Rumania, for example, the
Russians have supported the inclusion in the government of
out-and-out Fascist like Tatarescu."

For the first time the major glanced nervously around the
plane to see whether anyone was listening to our conversation.
I don't think they were. I guess he decided the same thing.

"Rumania? We are not discussing Rumania. In Germany
I can tell you about one item after another. Who is this
Doctor Mueller* you support in Bavaria? Democrat? No,
he is Nazi sympathizer."

"I don't know much about Germany," I said.

"You don't know much about Germany? That is too bad.
You should. Was Rumania our main enemy in war? Yet you
know about Rumania, you say. Germany is point of danger
always. It is Germany we agreed to make democratic at
Potsdam? Yes? How is this carried out by you? Not very well,
I think. You Americans had better make it your business to
know about Germany."

"How much do you know about Japan?" I countered because I had nothing else to say and because my stomach was

*The reference is presumably to Dr. Josef Mueller, Chairman of the Chris-
tian Social Union in Bavaria. The claim that his party is infiltrated with
Nazi sympathizers has not been denied even by Mueller.

not staying very still. I wished the plane would be taken up a few thousand feet.

"Our responsibility in Japan is limited by your policy of running one whole show. Let us not go away from Germany. You know nothing about Germany, you say?"

"I do more reading than the average Russian," I said, testily. "I know that the Russians have encouraged the union of the Communist and Social Democratic parties in their zone into one unified party. That has not happened in the other zones, because the Socialists voted against unity."

"And you encouraged disunity. You do not realize it was that same disunity of working class parties in 1933 that helped Hitler seize power? No, you don't. Now you want disunity for fear workers will take power."

"I think we still believe in civil and political liberties," I said, "and I read stories in the American newspapers that indicate we don't think that such things exist in the Soviet zone."

"Propaganda," Sokolov snorted, "I tell you, propaganda. You do not believe this? Very good, I give you one example. In Schleswig-Holstein, British zone, German county deputies elected one Communist man as their *Landrat* (County Commissioner.) Did British approve this democratic election? They did not. Their military government appointed one Christian Democrat."

I was silent, concentrating on maintaining the equilibrium of my insides. There were too many people in the plane; too little air. The steady beat of the motors seemed to ricochet against my eardrums. It did not appear to bother the doughty Major.

"Do you want to know more about Germany? All right. Last week was held in Essen, British zone, one big political meeting organized by Unity Committee. They asked Wilhelm Pieck and Otto Grotewohl to speak. Did they speak? No. Why? British military government cannot grant them permission for travel in British zone. Yes, they are Communists. But *you* talked about your liberties. Liberty for what? You give liberties to which kinds of people? I will tell you. In Bad Kissingen, American zone, your officers collaborate not with workers. They might be Communists. So they find time to collaborate with one Prince Louis Ferdinand, pretender to German throne. Your political advisers have not time for talks with German underground leaders. They prefer former Crown Prince Wilhelm von Hohenzollern. Do not talk to Sokolov about liberties."

In our embassy news bulletin in Moscow I had read a report of Red Army terror against Social Democrats. I mentioned this to Sokolov. He did not make a direct denial. "Some certain Social Democrats we do not trust just because they hide behind working class party. Perhaps it is true. I do not know. But do you know that Germans openly joke that your geh-too (United States Army G-2, intelligence branch) is little name for geh-stapoo?" He offered me a Kazbek *papirossi* which I quickly refused. "Two lieutenants on my staff have disappeared in Berlin now for two weeks. Where are they? Ask geh-too. You have double-faces, you Americans. What Rusians do is terrible. What British do is exceptional case. What Americans do is buried in one coffin part of mind behind what Russians do and what British do."

After a while the air became less bumpy and I began to feel better. I asked Sokolov if he thought there would be war with America.

"No," he said. "Not unless you attack us."

"Do you think we would ever do a thing like that?"

He frowned. "Why else do you go on spending billions of dollars to build new atom bombs? For defense?" Then he launched into a pattern of ideas which had become familiar by now: Churchill's Fulton speech, Truman's anti-labor legislation, America's insistence on retaining sole rights to the atom bomb, the Anglo-American bloc, the death of Roosevelt and what it meant to Russians. When he had finished I asked, "Has Russia discovered the secret of the atom bomb?"

"I don't know."

"You probably don't know this, either," I said, "but are you trying to make an atom bomb?"

Sokolov appeared genuinely surprised. "What for? We are not going to attack anyone."

Then I asked him what about Russian spies in Canada and reports that the Russians were experimenting with rockets in their zone of Germany.

"I admit nothing," he said. "Naturally our army does not go to sleep. Our Socialist motherland is always in danger and we must be prepared to defend ourselves. Don't you think we must know what weapons our potential enemies have to use against us? Certainly."

After a silence I asked the Major how the Red Army men liked the German girls. He did not reply and I thought perhaps he had not heard me. I repeated the question. He replied with a show of irritation.

"That is typical question of typical American journalist. Someone asked me once what time General Kotikov sleeps. This is to my mind childish and ridiculous and I do not even listen to you."

Major Sokolov never spoke to me again.

The "Secret" Airport

At five forty-five the plane landed at a small airdrome near Berlin. I wanted to make a telephone call but had to wait while several Red Army men tried manfully to make dates, with, I presume, German girls in a mixture of German and Russian.

The busy Russian in charge of the bare reception room in the little airport said she would summon a car to take me to Berlin. How long? Ten minutes. After twenty minutes I asked her again and stood next to her while she called the Red Army motor pool. Ten minutes more, she reported. A half hour later the car still had not arrived and she telephoned again. "Ask if it has been dispatched," I said.

It hadn't. Then I tried to reach my office in Berlin. A connection was finally achieved through three or four switchboards and I made my presence known. They promised to send a car. The Russian girl assured me a Russian car was on its way. An hour elapsed and nothing happened. I went back to the girl and asked to be shown to the Soviet commandant of the field. All the other passengers on the plane had long since departed from the airport by bus and auto.

The girl looked genuinely troubled. "Why don't you take a taxi?" she suggested.

"Isn't that what I've been awaiting for almost two hours?"

"Oh, no. I sent for a limousine. You are a foreign official and you should have the best. But it is so late. I am so sorry."

"How quickly can I get a taxi?"

"Right away."

In less than five minutes a taxi appeared, and I rode off to Berlin. There I talked with Masha Scott, the Russian-born wife of *Time's* Berlin Correspondent, John Scott.

Masha reported. "After you called I did not know where to send the car. I telephoned the colonel in charge of the airport. I told him in Russian that I wanted to send a car for you and would he please give me the address. Do you know what he said? He said he could not tell me the address, that the location of the Russian airport was a military secret. I said that you were coming in on a Russian plane from Moscow and that you would know where the airport was so how could it be a secret. But the colonel persisted. It must remain a secret. He hung up. I telephoned again and asked him to give you this address if he would not reconsider and tell me where the airport was. He would not tell me. By the way, where *is* the secret airport?"

"Just outside of Schoenfeld," I said.

"My God," said Masha, "what a secret! That's the American zone."

PART VI

THE DWINDLING PEACE

I WAS prepared for it. But still it was a shock to arrive in Paris, after a trip across Russia, and find Americans there talking about war with the Soviet Union as though it were as inevitable as next June. Not just any Americans: cabinet members, senior senators, journalists of repute and, of course, the military men. You asked them, "Are we going to attack Russia?" They, in turn, put on a politely shocked expression; that is, all except the military men, who have not discarded the idea of "getting it over now." "No, no," said the others, "but Russia is militant and belligerent, Russia is expanding, Russia is threatening, Russia wants. . . ."

Whether Russia wants war or not is opinion. The plain truth is that Russia is in no condition to start or conduct a major war of any kind, much less a war that would involve the United States. This is the hard core of economic fact—socialist or capitalist—despite the bellowing of *Pravda*, the inscrutability of Mr. Molotov, the obstructionism of Mr. Gromyko, the acidity of Mr. Vishinsky. "Oh, we know the

Russian *people* don't want war," our bigwigs hasten to set the public record straight, "but their dictatorship. . . ."

The Kremlin is full of towers but none of them are ivory. The realistic men who inhabit the Kremlin's towers know what's going on. They may be poorly informed on conditions in other nations, but at least they know that their own country is in bad shape, industrially and agriculturally. They know that their people are strained to the point of exhaustion, physically and nervously. They know that—at least until Churchill's speech at Fulton—there was plenty of grumbling. They used that speech to solidify their home front. With slackening of wartime controls, corruption and inefficiency have spread. Because criticism was discouraged, if not stifled, during the war years, many party bureaucrats solidified their hold, grew away from the rank and file. Now there is a vast *chistka* or clean-up going on in Russia. Party bosses who have failed to produce are being thrown out, not so much because of direction from above but because of pressure from below. Industrial managers, who were extremely well-rewarded during the war, became accustomed to easy living, too easy living. To keep their bonuses and premiums rolling in they falsified production reports, offered and accepted graft. Today they are being cleaned out—despite the fact that the country has a crying need for experienced managers.

The men in the Kremlin know all these things. So does the American Ambassador, General Bedell Smith. The material is openly published in the Soviet newspapers for all to read. The answer to those who yammer "We know the Russian *people* don't want war, but their dictatorship . . ." is simple.

THE DWINDLING PEACE

The Soviet leaders, no matter how strong or popular, no matter how completely they are in control of press, Party and people, could not lead their people into a new war except in self-defense.

The American people have an inflated notion about the strength of the Soviet Union. The delusion is inspired partly by the Red Army's magnificent victories, by Soviet propaganda, and by careless writing on the subject of Russia which confuses *present* and *potential* Soviet power.

The true facts are these:

In 1941 Stalin said that in 1957 Soviet per capita production of iron, steel, coal, and oil would equal that of the United States as it was in 1929. Since then the industrial gap between ourselves and Russia has been widened even further. Four years of war's destruction set back the Soviet Union at least five years, while the impetus of war production spurred United States industrial capacity far beyond the previous 1929 high. For example, Soviet pig iron production will not again reach the Russian prewar top (when it was third to the United States and Britain) until 1949. In 1946 Russia had the capacity to produce fifteen million tons of steel; capacity production in the United States is eighty-nine million tons.

What is true of iron and steel is true of other basic commodities. On February 9, 1946 at the Bolshoi Theater, in what was called a "warlike" speech by some United States commentators, Stalin publicly revealed the weakness of Russia's position when he announced to the world the Soviet economic blueprint for the future: the fourth Five-Year

Plan. This is a blueprint which needs peace, not war, for its
realization. Stalin said that in a *minimum* of fifteen years the
Soviet Union would attempt to treble its industrial production. If these goals are achieved, it will still leave the U.S.S.R.
far short of capacities which the United States has already
attained:

	U.S.S.R.-1960	U.S.A.-1944-45
Pig Iron	50 million tons per year	61 million tons per year
Steel	60 million tons per year	89 million tons per year
Coal	500 million tons per year	684 million tons per year
Oil	60 million tons per year	229 million tons per year

*   *   *

The Soviet people, in addition to being ill-housed, are also
ill-clothed and ill-fed. There has been almost no shoe production in the Soviet Union, except for the armed forces, for five
years. Now there are shoes available but the boots of army
men are wearing out. The total output has been so inadequate
that it could not supply *half* the people in the Soviet Union
with one new pair of shoes during 1946.

The war sharply curtailed production of textiles for clothing. Practically one-half of the flax fields were in areas
occupied by the Germans, and in the first year of liberation
the crop was only forty per cent of normal.

The bulk of Soviet cotton was grown in the Ukraine, the
Caucasus, and in Uzbekistan, in Central Asia. The Ukrainian
and Caucasian cotton is just beginning to come back and
production in all areas this year will only be up to sixty per
cent of prewar levels. Because of the need for beet sugar (the

Ukrainian supply was wiped out) some of the Uzbek cotton fields had to be replanted with beets. The shortage was increased by lack of manpower, tractors and seeds.

The Russian food situation also continues to be far below prewar standards. In 1946 the Russians had less meat than in 1940 because the Soviet Union, as a result of the war, was left with twenty-five per cent less cattle, forty per cent less sheep, sixty per cent less hogs. In addition the manpower shortage on the farms kept cattle raising in check. Food rationing in the Soviet Union is continuing in 1947 instead of having ended in 1946 due to "drought in a number of regions and the diminishing of State food reserves."

Despite the export of token shipments of grain to Poland and France, largely for political reasons, the 1946 crops were unequal to those of 1940. The same is true of sugar. The Germans held areas which gave eighty-seven per cent of the sugar used in Russia. In 1945 sugar beet production was at thirty per cent of normal; in 1946 it could only be stepped up to fifty per cent of the prewar total.

The men in the Kremlin know all these things. Last year Stalin told a Congressional group from the House of Representatives that, if credits were made available, the U.S.S.R. would purchase one million tons of foodstuffs from the United States. But the credits were not forthcoming.

Some of these pressing economic deficiencies help to explain Soviet actions in other countries.

The Russians have been accused of stealing cattle, "liberating" vehicles, ripping up rail ties from their zones in Europe, especially in Germany. Such charges are undoubtedly true but exaggerated. However we, thousands of miles from the reality, tend to forget or ignore the fact that the Germans destroyed more Russian cattle, farm machinery and tracks than there are in *all* of Germany.

The United States has access to all the oil it can use in peacetime; the Soviet Union badly needs oil. So badly that Soviet merchant ships were tied up in Vladivostok Harbor for lack of fuel. During the war years Soviet oil wells were improperly cared for, because maintenance engineers were urgently required at the front and new equipment could not be manufactured. The output at Baku, the largest oil area, slumped badly. This is one reason why the Soviets have pursued an aggressive oil policy in Iran, Austria, Hungary and Rumania. For although an idealistic phrase in the Atlantic Charter pledged equal access to world markets, Russia found the quickest and most realistic "access" was by expropriation.

Add to the lack of housing, clothing and food an antiquated navy and a shipbuilding capacity which will reach six hundred thousand tons by 1950 (our capacity is eighteen million tons a year), and the Soviet Union appears less of an immediate military threat. Its air force, while a good tactical arm of the army, is not a potent attacking force. To date, the Russians have not specialized in building long-range bombers as we have.

And the Russians do not have the atom bomb, without which no nation is likely to wage an aggressive major war today or tomorrow.

THE DWINDLING PEACE

Casting the First Atom

Since August 13, 1945, the nations of the world who won the war have been struggling to win the peace. It has not been an easy task: nations that were unified by a common cause against a common enemy found little unity in their separate quests for peace. The United Nations formed an organization in San Francisco dedicated to the theory that everyone wanted peace. But the intervening months have demonstrated that not every nation wants the same peace or wants to employ the same methods to insure that peace.

Specifically the two states which emerged from the war more influential than any others, the United States and the U.S.S.R., have failed to agree on either the theory or practice of peace. World War II set the wheel of history spinning rapidly toward social revolution. The Soviets recognized this fact and sought, by force when necessary, to channelize the revolution along Soviet or pro-Soviet lines. Hesitantly, we watched the wheel spin before we recognized where it was going; then we stepped in and tried to stop it. That was not leadership, not the kind of leadership the people of Europe wanted or needed. In most states the Communists were not in the majority. If we had recognized the fact of social revolution without gagging on the terminology we could have supplied positive leadership: dynamic democracy. Instead of that we mistakenly decided that the only thing to do was to check the wheel, check Russia. If they appealed to the Left, we would appeal to the Right. The Soviets went to the other extreme, alienated many middle-of-the-road anti-Fascist

groups in Europe by their tactics. Similar goals which
Americans shared with the Russians were forgotten or ignored; differences were emphasized by both sides. As a result
it must be evident even to the most ardent and sincere
champions of the rights of little nations that unless the Big
Two can continue to compromise their differences and con-
solidate their similarities *this is only an interim peace.*

The glow of American-Soviet top-level co-operation which
reached its brightest at Yalta has almost completely faded.
From the Russian viewpoint, the chief reason for this cooling-
off was the Anglo-American decision, voiced in no uncertain
terms by President Truman on October 8, 1945, that we
would not share the secret of the atom bomb with our wartime allies.

The Russians ask: what is the use of talking about friendship, mutual trust and military co-operation within the
United Nations when one nation or group controls the
mightiest weapon of war ever devised and withholds it from
the other side?

It is not patriotic to yell, "Give the bomb to Russia" unless
you mean "give" in the sense of "let 'em have it." Neither
is it logical to yell, "Would they have given it to us?" The fact
is that we have discovered, perfected and used the bomb;
therefore, the responsibility for its future is ours.

Professor Albert Einstein and others have declared, not
without reason, that if President Roosevelt had lived we
might not have used the bomb we did. Our military chiefs
in Washington had a pretty good idea that the Japanese were

practically through in the summer of 1945. The debate on whether to use the bomb on Hiroshima and Nagasaki was considerable. The deciding argument was: "Let's end it fast before the Russians grab too much."

Once having employed the bomb, the United States could have immediately signified its willingness to place control of atomic energy in the hands of the United Nations' Security Council. The very American scientists who developed the atom bomb publicly stated that another power which so desired could develop the bomb in "not more than a few years." Therefore, unless the United States was committed in advance to a policy of possible diplomatic or military aggression against the Soviet Union within that limited period of years, we had little to lose by sharing the secret.

We had the world to gain by sharing it.

Only with this gesture—the greatest single contribution to world peace and security that one nation could have made— might we have been able to disintegrate the Russian "neurosis" about capitalist encirclement. Then perhaps the isolation-minded members of the Politburo (led by Molotov) might have been outvoted, and the Russian people would have had sufficient proof that the Soviet Union was in the family of nations on a permanent basis. Instead, the converse occurred.

President Truman and his board of strategy may have decided to hold onto the secret of atomic fission for another reason. If properly developed, atomic energy has great potential peacetime uses, one of which is cheap power. As Peter Kapitza, the Soviet Union's foremost atomic physicist, recently put it, "To talk of atomic energy only in terms of atomic bombs is like talking of electricity in terms of the electric chair." He believes that the Soviet Union, with no commitments to private capital, could put atomic energy to work for the people in the vastness of Siberia, in the marshes of Byelorussia, in the plains of the Ukraine, in the valleys of the Urals and the hot plateaus of Central Asia. The Soviet standard of living might rise, sharply and quickly. The Soviet economy would then become more attractive to the impoverished peoples of Europe, according to Kapitza.

In June 1946, ten months after the explosion over Hiroshima, the United States offered the Baruch Plan for the control of the atom bomb to the United Nations' Atomic Energy Commission. This occurred during my stay in Moscow. As an American who believes in full public discussion of such important issues, I thought that the Soviet press should have published the report. Instead only official criticism of the Baruch Plan appeared.

While condemning their failure to permit the publication of the plan, I could understand their failure to become enthusiastic about it. Behind *Pravda's* barrage of charges, there were two major Soviet objections which Russians in Moscow pointed out to me. Primarily the Russians were afraid that under the Baruch Plan the establishment of a UN control body (Atomic Development Authority) would be in slow stages; and that while they and other nations were handing over their raw materials and research (which is probably considerable), the United States would be left with a "monopoly " of atomic bombs. The counterplan proposed by Andrei Gromyko, Soviet delegate to the UN, called for "atomic disarmament" prior to the setting up of controls rather than afterward.

Possibly the Russians might have been less suspicious of our motives and more willing to compromise if the Baruch Plan had been presented six months earlier. But by midsummer 1946 the Russians were charging that our navy and air force had become arms of American foreign policy; i.e., in Turkey and Greece. Some Russians even speculated on when the atomic bomb would be used as a threat. We Americans argue that such a step is not morally possible for the United States. Yet an important aspect of international relations is the effect our moves have on others; and the Russians see "atomic diplomacy" as a natural growth of our current policy.

From another standpoint, the Russians felt that the Baruch Plan might delay or prevent the employment of atomic energy in the Soviet Union for peacetime purposes. Since the process of producing atomic energy is the same, up to a point, for destruction or for development, the American international control plan could (with a majority vote by other nations) obstruct industrial uses of nuclear fission in any one country. And the Russians believe, rightly or wrongly, that their country would become, by its very nature, the first to convert to a peacetime use of atomic energy.

My trip through Russia has reaffirmed my belief that the people of the Soviet Union, and most of their responsible leaders, sincerely desire peace. How many of the leaders now believe that peace is possible I do not know. Until the death of Roosevelt and the use of the atom, they were in the majority and Stalin was on their side. Since then they have been very much on their guard against a Third World War although still eager for peace. Everything bespeaks it—Molotov's truculence in Paris, Stalin's speeches in Moscow. On March 22, 1946 the Soviet premier renounced any desire for war and declared, "I attach great importance to the United Nations organization, as it is a serious instrument for the preservation of peace and international security." Little more than a month later, on May Day, Stalin warned that, while the Soviet Union would be true to its policy of peace and security, the Russian people must not "forget for a single minute the intrigues of international reaction which are hatching plans for a new war."

As Russia Sees Us

This is an *apologia* for Russia only in the sense that it is a plea for us to examine our own sins as well as Russia's. We know theirs all too well. The press harps on them, real and imagined, every day. The Russian people know our sins, real and imagined, too. "Until we are taught what our history books do not teach," says Professor Einstein, "—that the fault is usually ours quite as much as some other nations —we have not taken the first step to that wisdom which alone can save us."

This step we, as leaders, must take first. Eventually the Soviet Union and all nations must follow. The great obstacle to this step lies in the fact that here, as in the Soviet Union, a new self-righteous nationalism has arisen side by side with the need for internationalism. The furor raised in the United States over Henry Wallace's plea for a re-examination of our Russian policy is a case in point. In his letter to President Truman on that subject, Wallace posed this question: "How do American actions since V-J Day appear to other nations? I mean by actions the concrete things like $13,000,000,000 for the War and Navy Departments, the Bikini tests of the atomic bomb and continued production of bombs, the plan to arm Latin America with our weapons, production of B-29's and planned production of B-36's and the effort to secure air bases spread over half the globe from which the other half of the globe can be bombed. I cannot but feel that these actions must make it look to the rest of the world as if we were only paying lip service to peace at the conference table."

For proposing that America be prepared to criticize itself as well as Russia, Wallace was branded by many newspapers and politicians as an "appeaser" and an "idealist." He was eventually dropped from the Truman cabinet for voicing in a public address what he had previously written to the President privately; and for expressing views, as a cabinet member, which disagreed with United States policy.

The United States has a "unified" foreign policy. Senator Vandenberg likes it and so does Senator Connally. On domestic issues they do not see eye to eye. The Republican is against certain concepts in domestic life which the Democrat approves. But in foreign policy today there is almost no concept at work on which they can disagree; the foreign policy of the United States boils down to "stop Russia." This policy may not lead ultimately to war. The important thing is that it does not lead ultimately to a real basis for peace.

THROUGH RUSSIA'S BACK DOOR

The maze in which the world finds itself did not just happen. We, along with the Russians, had the responsibility of supplying leadership for the peace as we supplied it in the war. We fell on our collective and rugged individualist faces. We blamed the Russians; they blamed us.

As divergencies grew, we labeled the Security Council veto power as the Russian-conceived hatchet of Russian obstructionism. Forgotten in the American press and radio was the fact that at San Francisco we were equally firm about the veto power because the American representatives feared that the United States Senate would not accept United Nations membership without it. It is true, however, that we have not abused the veto as Russia has by stifling discussion; but we did use the veto against the proposal to withdraw recognition of Franco in Spain.

While we built new atom bombs at home, some have ranted about the size of Russia's army and Russia's expenditures for armaments. In 1946 Russia has been allocating about forty per cent of her budget for military expenditures*; and so have we. The total of military expenditures by the so-called Anglo-American bloc is far greater than that of the Soviet Union and its so-called bloc.

Scare headlines have blackened the better newspapers when a Red Army troop movement was rumored. If Americans become that worked up over a rumor, how must the Russian people feel about our dress rehearsal at Bikini? "The experiments at Bikini mean suspicion of our purposes," writes

* The latest Soviet budget, announced on October 16, 1946, lists only twenty-three per cent for the armed forces—a drastic reduction in Russia's military expenditures.

ex-Secretary of the Interior Harold Ickes. "They mean rivalry generated by desperation; they mean more tests, more bombs and more tests until that hapless day when the reckless misuses of God's power explode and sweep us all into the rubble-littered dustpan of oblivion."

Actually the Bikini tests were watered-down; the bombs dropped were not as powerful as those which smeared death over Japan. Perhaps it was to lull Russian fears; more likely it was to help maintain large appropriations for naval vessels which are now somewhat less than vital to United States military might. If Russia had flexed her atomic muscles in tests near the Aleutians—then Americans really would have cause for concern about the future of the world's peace.

Among the most bitter and one-sided critics of Russia today are former sycophants of Wendell Willkie's concept of One World. They believe that Soviet nationalism and Soviet imperialism alone has split the one world into two.

As the Russian sees it, Anglo-American diplomacy has an equal if not greater responsibility for that split. Churchill's speech struck a mighty blow for the great division.

In their eyes the United States has made as many strange bedfellows abroad as we think the Russians have. On the question of the Dardanelles we have been backing Turkey, our enemy in World War I and a non-ally in World War II. The Russians feel they ought to have a great deal to say about the straits, which they believe are as vital to the defense of the Soviet Union as the Suez Canal appears to be to Great Britain's or the Panama Canal to ours.

In Spain, the Russians feel we have soft-pedaled opposition to Franco.

In Indonesia, they say we have blinked at the oppression of colonial peoples because to take a stand might weaken our teamwork with the British. The Soviets point out that the same has been true of our lack of an affirmative policy in Palestine where Britain's thirst for oil has pushed the Labor Government into the strange position of backing Arab feudalism.

In China, Russians correctly recall that we dedicated ourselves to helping the establishment of a democratic government and the widening of democracy; but they point out, because the most reactionary men in the Kuomintang correctly analyzed the "stop Russia" principle as the rock in the snowball of our foreign policy, these pro-war Kuomintang leaders have paid slight attention to the peace-making efforts of General George C. Marshall and Ambassador J. Leighton Stuart.*

In Greece, the Russians believe that the British—with ourselves as silent partners—pushed the wheel of history backwards by supporting Tories and Royalists who collaborated with Fascism; by suppressing the largest resistance movement (EAM) in the name of checking the growth of Communism.†

For a complete summary of how the Russians have been seeing us and the rest of the world, the reader is referred to Appendices A, B, and C.

---

* For a report on our role in China, see *Thunder Out of China* by Annalee Jacoby and Theodore H. White.

† For a report on the Allied role in Greece, see pp. 242-270 of *While Time Remains* by Leland Stowe.

THE DWINDLING PEACE

The democrats of all parties who have so easily given up one world and have settled for two, maintain that Democracy, as we understand it, and Communism cannot live and work side by side. Even Henry Wallace implied this in his New York speech on September 12, 1946, when he said: "We should recognize that we have no more business in the political affairs of Eastern Europe than Russia has in the political affairs of Latin America, Western Europe and the United States." This is, in effect, accepting an armed peace—two worlds.

The argument for a permanent split rather than coalition frequently cites the open civil war in China and the undeclared struggles in Poland. I have been in both these countries and have seen their one-sided governments at work. In China, despite our protestations of disinterested fatherly love for the Chinese people and our desire to help them achieve democracy, United States policy has been the ultimate backing which keeps the Kuomintang from giving the Communists the share in the government which their influence and mass following warrant. In Poland, despite Russia's expressed desire for a free, strong and democratic Poland, Soviet policy has been the ultimate backing which has permitted the Warsaw Government to keep Stanislas Mikolajczyk's relatively conservative Peasant Party from exerting the influence which its following warranted.

If American and Soviet policy could be broadened, if mutual faith between the Big Two could be restored, both China and Poland would be able to achieve a greater degree of democracy. When American or Soviet policy is not the predetermining factor other parties can work with the Communists. In France, considered in the so-called Western orbit, and in Czechoslovakia, in the Eastern, the United States and the Soviet Union have maintained relatively a hands-off policy. In both nations the Communist Party has a leading role and has worked with other large, responsible parties without violence.

If the divergent philosophies can be harnessed to work for France and Czechoslovakia, then there is still hope for one world. That is, always providing that the United States and the Soviet Union strive effectively enough under the United Nations harness. The first step would be, on our part, an immediate reshaping of our foreign policy, a willingness and an ability to offer the world a more positive program for lasting peace than "stop Russia." It might be initiated by a Big Three or Big Two meeting in which we declared and were prepared to implement our determination not to attack Russia (they cannot possibly attack us), our desire to become friends with Russia, to assist their rehabilitation with a loan, to settle atomic control without holding onto a stockpile of bombs, to fight fascism wherever it exists or crops up. Friendship is, of course, a mutual relationship. We can only hope that the Soviet Union will accept the extended hand as they did during World War II.

Premier Stalin's answers to questions put to him by Alexander Werth last September certainly indicate the Soviet leader's willingness to talk peace (see Appendix C). In one question, Correspondent Werth asked bluntly, "Do you believe in the possibility of a friendly and lasting collaboration of the Soviet Union and Western Democracy despite the existence of ideological discord, and in friendly competition between the two systems . . . ?"

Stalin replied, "I do, unconditionally."

While a coalition world is possible under the United Nations, it should be obvious that we are still a long way from the dream of world federation.

The Double Standard

A year before he died, Wendell Willkie stated: "Russia is neither going to eat us nor seduce us. . . . The best answer to Communism is a living, vibrant, fearless democracy—economic, social and political. All we need to do is to stand up and perform according to our professed ideals."

That is a good basis for formulating a foreign policy. It is unworthy of us to put up one brand of democracy for the North and one for the South, one for export and one for import. If the American brand includes land reform in Japan and Korea, why not in China and Germany? If it opposes the suppression of rights of the opposition in Eastern Europe, why not oppose it in Greece, Spain, Indonesia and Palestine?

A good deal that Soviet journalist and propagandist Ilya Ehrenburg writes or says is as emotional and subjective in its way as Dorothy Thompson is in hers. But in his *Collier's* article which appeared during his visit to the United States, Ehrenburg wrote with some degree of relevancy and truth that American newspapers have double standards—"one for virtuous United States and Great Britain and the other for sinful Russia."

"If the Americans consider Iceland their base, then it is a 'guarantee of world security.' If the Soviet Union does not want her neighboring states to be used as bases of aggression against Russia, then it is 'red imperialism.'

"If Americans produce atomic bombs, it is the abstract work of scientists or an innocent pastime like football. If Red Army men walk in formation along a Moscow street to the steam baths, that is 'preparation for a Third World War.' "

The "stop Russia" policy of our State Department has found strong backing among correspondents, editors and newspaper. I have seen reporters in the Orient dig up or cook up anti-Russian angles for their stories to make page one. If the American press has done an honest job of informing its readers about Russia, the public's knowledge of the Soviet Union wouldn't prove it.

According to a recent Elmo Roper poll in *Fortune*, sixty-six per cent of the people in the United States were either uninformed or badly informed about the U.S.S.R.; only twelve per cent were well informed and twenty-two per cent fairly well informed.

Not only have the American public an unclear picture of Russia's role in the world today, but they can remember little about Russia's prewar position in international affairs. They know about the Nazi-Soviet pact because newspapers remind them of it. But, according to a poll taken by the National Opinion Research Center at the University of Denver, only 13.4 per cent of the public was aware that the Soviet Union sympathized with Ethiopia rather than Italy (73 per cent did not know); only 14.4 per cent realized that

Russian sympathies were with the Czechs when Germany threatened that country just before the war (58 per cent did not know).

In the first six months of 1946 over ninety per cent of the reading public in America believed that Russia was the main obstacle on the problem of unifying Germany; actually it was France which for a long time balked at even discussion of the subject. There are many other examples which would support the Ehrenburg charge. And the fact that Russia's press is biased is no excuse for us. For we are the upholders of the fair and free press.

Scarcely a day passes that the "double standard" does not show up in the press. Sometimes it is by intent, sometimes by negligence, sometimes by omission. Perhaps the greatest sin is omission. News is based primarily on trouble and conflict: murder, divorce, fire, battles, rape, etc. Normal deaths, marriages, births and the completion of apartment houses (rather than their destruction) are reported but they are less likely to become page one items. Thus in the field of international relations the bitter discords are bannered, the accords lightly dismissed or omitted. For the same reason a turbulent election in Poland rates more space than a peaceful one in Czechoslovakia, even though the results of the Czech balloting may be just as important in the long run to the newspaper reader as the results in Warsaw.

On many international committees and undertakings the United States and the Soviet Union have bickered; these quarrels are headlined. At the Nurnberg trials, for example, I am told that the justices and lawyers of the two nations worked together with surprising smoothness. This never rated a front page story or even a column from the hard-up international pundits who drew dire conclusions from each new American-Soviet verbal fracas.

As this chapter is being written, the newspapers are liberally sprinkled with instances of the "double standard" which would make Ehrenburg's eyes sparkle. The day-to-day reporting on the United Nations could supply almost daily examples. The United States turned down the U.N. applications of Albania and Outer Mongolia with the assertion that they were "puppet" states and sponsored by the Soviet Union. Nothing was said by our State Department, and very little by the press comments, about American support for the British-sponsored applications of Trans-Jordania and Portugal. It would be difficult to prove that these two nations were less puppet than the Soviet-sponsored regimes. The only excuse the press has on this is that their "double standard" is identical with the State Department's.

As a final example, this is how non-conflict stories can be buried. On September 2, 1946, the New York *Times* published this tiny item on the bottom of the last page of its first section.

SAYS U.S. TAKES NAZI BAIT

Colgate Man Decries Blaming
Russia For All World Ills

HAMILTON, N.Y. SEPT. 1—Americans are following the Nazi propaganda line laid down by Dr. Joseph Goebbels when they blame the Russians for all international woes Dr. Rod-

ney L. Mott, director of the Division of Social Sciences at
Colgate University, declared tonight in an address before
business, civic and educational leaders of this village.

"The only nation that has anything to gain from a quarrel
between the United States and Russia is Germany, and the
Germans are now making every effort to drive a wedge between the occupying powers in order to secure that advantage," Dr. Mott asserted.

Dr. Mott recently returned after having served with the
United States Military Government in Berlin as deputy
chief of the Finance Division of the Office of Military
Government.

The other New York City morning newspapers that day
did not publish this story at all. If an officer of the United
States Military Government in Berlin had returned and made
a speech denouncing Russia and placing the onus for the
world woes on the Soviets, his views probably would have
rated more space. That would have been news. I sometimes
wonder: Is it the kind of news people want to read or the
kind of news other people want to print?

The Last Chance

In the reaction which follows a great war there is always
a "smart" tendency to debunk its horrors. For a while this
assumed the form of analytical articles by military semi-
experts who did not concede that atomic energy has revolu-
tionized both war and peace.

The people of Japan, guinea pigs for the first atomic burst
at Hiroshima and Nagasaki, know better. Early in 1946 I
walked among them in the glazed rubble that was Hiroshima.

No individual with whom I talked had survived the disaster without the loss of close relatives, friends and possessions.

Photographs, no matter how precise, cannot portray the crumbling of blood cells as they can the crumbling of bricks, the twisting of men's souls as they can the twisting of steel girders. John Hersey's report, *Hiroshima,* told the story in human terms as well as it has ever been told.

The next Hiroshima—it may be Moscow or New York, Khabarovsk or Seattle, Nanking or Kansas City, Stockholm or New Orleans—will be far more horrible. No logic can argue as cogently for the necessity of making every effort to attain a durable peace as this single item: the atom bombs which fell on Japan in the summer of 1945 had the explosive power of 20,000 tons of dynamite; shortly after the war's conclusion, Oak Ridge had developed a new atom bomb which packed the explosive power of twenty million tons of dynamite. Even this may be obsolete by now.

The residue of peace and the time left for making a permanent peace is dwindling. The world is one physical body, but it has two mutually sensitive nerve centers. An American action in Japan might be the reason for a Soviet action in Austria; Soviet pressure on Iran can result in an American loan to Turkey; British policy in Greece may be reflected in Soviet policy in Rumania.

Wendell Willkie's One World still exists and it is shrinking, in the physical sense, every jet-propelled minute. Not even nuclear fission can split it physically. But it is a world with two minds. Unless its intensifying schizophrenia can be resolved, violent madness will result. The two nervous systems will destroy each other, leaving only a world of radio-active pulp and bones. This is our last chance.

*   *   *

No man realized the urgency of winning the peace more clearly than Franklin Delano Roosevelt. In his Fourth Inaugural Address, delivered on January 20, 1945, he talked of the lessons learned from the war and pledged that we would profit by them. "We have learned that we cannot live alone, at peace;" he said, "that our own well-being is dependent upon the well-being of other nations far away. We have learned that we must live as men, and not as ostriches, nor as dogs in the manger."

In high hope he added, "We have learned to be citizens of the world, members of the human community."

That is the greatest task of this generation.

PART VII

Appendix: As It Seems to Moscow

A.

STRUGGLE OF THE DEMOCRATIC FORCES FOR THE FINAL DEFEAT OF FASCISM

by F. N. Oleshchuko

(Note: This lecture, delivered on June 7, 1946 at the Dom Soyuzov in Moscow, is one of a series open to the general public on world affairs. The series is under the supervision of the Communist Party's lecture bureau. The attendance at this lecture was only about forty; most of the listeners were enthusiastic. At the conclusion of the talk, the audience was invited to ask questions. Someone got up and said, "Is it true that Earl Browder is well received by the government?" Oleshchuko replied, "I cannot answer that." Another questioner wanted to know how greatly the Communists influenced the new Labor government of England. Oleshchuko said, "Of course the forthcoming elections within the Labor Party may reveal changes, but at present the Communists have relatively little influence."
The lecture was audited, transcribed and translated by a member of the Joint Press Reading Service in Moscow, which is operated by the British and Americans.)

The defeat of Fascism by armed force has greatly weakened world reaction. Nonetheless, it cannot be said that the end of Fascism has been brought about. It continues to exist in every form. In Germany it still exists in the British, French and American zones, not only in isolated individuals, but in organized groups of hundreds and even thousands. In Japan the foundations of life which gave birth to Fascism have not even been touched. The Emperor's power is there, the industrial and financial interests survive, there has been no agrarian reform, etc. In China Fascism continues under the auspices of the Kuomintang. In France a Fascist party exists openly. In Italy there are tens of Fascist and neo-Fascist organizations and parties which are legal. Fascist movements exist in all of the so-called neutral countries which helped Hitler during the war. Spain, of course, is the chief remaining source of Fascist infection. The situation is more serious now because of the presence of Hitlerite cadres there.

There has, in addition, been a considerable expansion of Fascist ideology in the U.S.A. and Great Britain. In England there are a number of legally operating Fascist organizations, in part Catholic supported. General Fuller is still writing. In the U.S.A. Fascists are as active as ever. The names of Nye, Wheeler, Taft, Fish, Hoover, Lindbergh, etc., still figure prominently. Recently there has been a great deal of anti-Semitism in the U.S.A. The Imperialism of the U.S.A. is supported by many Fascist groups backed by religious organizations.

The only state where Fascism does not and cannot exist in any form whatsoever is the Soviet Union.

How can Fascism be detroyed? Some answer glibly that it can be destroyed only if capitalism is destroyed. This would present an extremely gloomy picture, however, since nobody, not even the Communist Parties in the U.S.A. and Great Britain, is looking to the overthrow of capitalism in the near future.

Fascism is a manifestation of capitalist society in its imperialistic phase. It arose during the last great crisis of Capitalism and is manifested in the destruction of democratic processes.

The fact is that in capitalist countries operating on a bourgeois political basis, various forms of political organization may co-exist. The relationship between the classes is the determining factor. History is made by people. The victory of Fascism before this war was the result not only of the development of capitalism, but of the weakening of the forces which oppose Fascism. The working class is the basic anti-Fascist force. If there had been a united anti-Fascist front, the war would have been impossible. The disunity of the workers was what enabled Fascism to triumph. But there is nothing inevitable about Fascism. Its strength or weakness depends on the relationships between classes in a society.

What is the situation now? Fascism is defeated, true. But the bourgeois-capitalist world still retains the sources which feed Fascism. The same contradictions continue to exist in capitalism as did before. The tendency to beat down the working class, struggle against democratic liberation movements in the liberated countries, oppose the wishes of socialist countries—all these are bourgeois-capitalist manifestations on the basis of which Fascism continues to exist.

The war brought great changes in the imperialist camp. The general result of the war was to weaken imperialism and capitalism. France, Italy and Germany, three great imperialisms, are all weakened. A great democratic movement exists in Bulgaria, Rumania, Hungary, Yugoslavia, Czechoslovakia and Finland. The power of the Soviet Union has greatly increased. It all adds up to a weakening of capitalism. Comrade Stalin said before the war that Fascism was merely a sign of the weakness of bourgeois society.

In Great Britain and the U.S.A., however, imperialism has grown stronger. These countries did not go through the rigors of war and suffered relatively little damage to their material existence, especially the U.S.A. Their participation in the war was largely limited to the contributions of their agriculture and industry. Monopoly capitalism grew stronger in the U.S.A. and is now showing a strong influence on the course of international relations.

The U.S.A. and Great Britain are now supporting Fascism in the hope of using it to fight democracy and the Soviet Union. There is, of course, a much greater menace in the U.S.A. because it emerged the strongest of all capitalist countries and imperialist circles in the U.S.A. are more and more preaching Fascist plans and methods. There is a new slogan in the U.S.A.: "The twentieth century is the American century." The imperialists consider they now have the weapon of economic pressure plus the atom bomb, which is the same sort of terror weapon that Nazi Germany relied on. In fact there is a great deal in the U.S.A. today which reminds us of Germany before the war, including the reliance on fantastic methods of destruction to achieve aims.

Thus, the conclusion is that Fascism can be defeated only by striking heavy blows against reaction, which feeds it and uses it as a weapon. The reactionary forces in the world are at present larger than the Fascist forces, and the next step is to weaken the reaction.

THROUGH RUSSIA'S BACK DOOR

One year has passed since the end of the war, and in not a single case has Fascism been able to crush a Democratic movement (with a notable exception). Only in Greece has democracy been stifled. It has not been decisively destroyed, of course. The people continue to exist, as well as the Communist and Socialist parties. The struggle becomes more acute all the time and it is apparent that the Greek people must go through a period of great torment before democracy is achieved in their country. Democracy was crushed in Greece not because it proved weaker than Fascism, but because Great Britain backed the Fascists.

Except for Greece, nowhere else has Fascism triumphed. In France and Italy the struggle against reaction is complicated. In France the reaction was headed by De Gaulle. His forced retirement was a triumph for democracy. In the most recent election the Communist Party received more votes than in the previous one. If democracy is as slow there as it is, it is because there is no unity among the democratic forces. In Italy the recent referendum showed a majority against the monarchy and the old regime. The Communist Party now occupies one of the first places. The factor of lack of unity is even more present among the democratic forces in Italy than in France. Victory would be easy in Italy if there were unity of the democratic forces.

The greatest democratic triumphs, however, have been in eastern and southeastern Europe. There is here a popular democracy based on the workers and peasants. The reaction has been overcome. Politically, basic changes have taken place. There has been agrarian reform and the elimination of landlordism; heavy industry has been nationalized, all of which is a great blow against reaction and Fascism. The recent Bulgarian elections were a triumph for democracy. The opposition had few votes and would have been even smaller without British and American support. In Rumania and Hungary the reaction is stronger, especially in Hungary which was a country totally owned by private capital. Elections will take place shortly in Poland, which has been going through democratization. One of the bright lights is Czechoslovakia, which showed just how fast a nation can forge ahead on the democratic road. The Communist Party is now in first place in Czechslovakia and the new government will be headed by it. The Czech Communist Party won its election without resorting to a bloc with other democratic parties, as was necessary in Bulgaria and Yugoslavia. Churchill stated that the Communist Parties were dictating in these blocs, but in Czechoslovakia the Communist Party stood by itself and won. Yugoslavia is today the best democracy in eastern Europe, and is really a people's power.

These great democratic triumphs mean a great blow has been struck against Fascism and reaction. This is part of the final moral and political destruction of Fascism.

There have been great Asiatic victories. New states have arisen: Korea is now independent and is evolving toward democracy; there is finally a Mongolian People's Republic. In China itself democracy has won very considerable victories. Over one hundred million people are now living under a democratic system which is quite different from life under the Kuomintang. This people's order is led by the Chinese

Communist Party. It is supported by a people's army which did great service against the Japanese and is now struggling against Chiang Kai-shek. The people's movement in China has reached such proportions that the Kuomintang cannot crush it.

In Iran the Azerbaidzhan people, the most advanced of the population are on their way to democratic independence.

The democratic movements in the U.S.A. and Great Britain are not as strong as they are in Europe and Asia. There are historical factors helping to explain this. There has never been a tradition of left radical parties in these two countries. In the U.S.A. there is no strong influence being exercised by the Communist Party. In addition, the ruling classes in the U.S.A. and Great Britain have strengthened their positions as a result of the victory over Germany.

But what is taking place in the U.S.A. at the moment shows that the class struggle is growing more tense. There has been a series of labor conflicts and strikes, involving millions of workers and disrupting all the economic life of the country for weeks. The struggle against reaction and Fascism grows more bitter. The fact that the Case Bill passed and that a bill such as Truman's was even suggested, is good evidence of the intensified struggle in the U.S.A. These things are taking place in the citadel of imperialism.

The conclusion that must be drawn is that all over the world democratic forces have become so strong that all plans of the reaction against democracy have failed. Democracy is on the upsurge and winning virtually all over.

The strength of world Democracy today is based on the existence of the Soviet Union which is the opposite pole to the U.S.A. and Great Britain in the struggle against reaction. The Soviet Union plays a great role in the sense that in no case has it interfered with the development of democracy. Nowhere does it stand in the way of the masses building their own society. The others, that is, the U.S.A. and Great Britain, are doing everything in their power to hinder the development of democracy. Secondly, the role of the Soviet Union lies in supporting the national liberation movements of peoples all over the world, and in extending active aid to democratic movements in countries on her borders and elsewhere. In the case of Poland, this aid extended to assistance with arms, the Soviet Union agreeing to outfit the Polish army. Thirdly, the role of the Soviet Union lies in supporting these democratic movements at international conferences.

The Soviet Union is one of the initiators of the Charter of the United Nations. It feels that international co-operation must be based on unanimous agreements on major issues. It has brought up the issues of Greece and Spain in an effort to show that it is impossible to build lasting peace unless we get rid of the Fascists who brought on this war. The Soviet Union energetically defends the principle of international co-operation, without which peace is impossible. The Soviet Union is prepared to make compromises when necessary, but not on principles.

The fact that the Soviet Union emerged from the war as the greatest power in the world and is constantly growing stronger has resulted in strengthening democracy in the world. If unity were to be accomplished among working men, there is no doubt that the forces of reaction could be beaten.

B.

THE LESSONS OF THE WAR

by Academician Eugene Tarle

(Note: On June 22, 1946 this article appeared in Red Star, the official newspaper of the Red Army. It is written by Academician Tarle, considered by the Soviets to be their most distinguished historian. A few days after this article appeared Tarle was awarded a Stalin Prize for his historical writings. His analysis of the world situation represents not an official interpretation but one which probably does not differ in any important respect from the official interpretation. Every American should study it carefully to understand the Soviet viewpoint on the events of the past five years.)

Today is five years from the moment when the Hitlerite brigand band invaded the Soviet Union with the firm intention and complete certainty that not later than September 1941 the victorious "blond Siegfrieds," having conquered Russia and turned over all future problems connected with it to Alfred Rosenberg, "Director for the Region of the East" (*Oberbefehlshaber des Ostraumes*), would return home and march triumphantly under Berlin's Brandenburg Gates.

What made the Germans so very certain? It was not merely the high degree of preparedness of their armed forces. No— another phenomenon played an enormous role in this connection. A phenomenon which was at that time psychologically completely unavoidable.

What had preceded the attack on Russia? Two years of bloodless and painless victories for the German armies over almost all the countries of Continental Europe.

We now know very exactly, from their own testimonials,

228

that the Germans themselves had not expected such unbe-
lievable success for their "Fifth Columns."

One more effort only had to be made. Not "the last," but
the first real effort. It remained to defeat Russia.

"If not on September first then on September fifteenth we
shall be in Moscow," said Goebbels and the radio commentators under him.

"Russian resistance may still continue to November,"
people in America and Britain, even those friendly towards
us, were stating during the summer of 1941 when we were
going through such difficult battles.

"The rising of Europe against Bolshevism is taking place
very successfully!" exalted the traitorous French press in
Laval's Paris.

The Hoover and Scripps-Howard press warned Roosevelt
against intervening in a cause that was already lost.

But if the first lesson of history, the outcome of the policy
of Messrs. Chamberlain and Daladier, and of the treachery
of the fascist "Fifth Columns" was the enslavement by Hitler
Germany of almost all the European states, the second lesson
unlooked for by many public figures in Europe and Amercia,
was the powerful and uncrushable resistance of the Soviet
Union, firm as a granite cliff.

We here in Russia had not the slightest doubts even in
those first hard months of the war: it would all end not only
with driving out the barbaric hordes which had invaded our
country, but with the complete annihilation of the Fascist
Empire. Two hundred million people inhabiting our land
from the Niemen to the Pacific Ocean, from the Arctic

Ocean to Iran and India, agreed with heart and mind with this clear Stalin program. Throughout all history there has never been such unity of an entire people around its leader. Four years passed—and Germany lay crushed and under the heel of the conquerors. This was the second lesson of history.

Only one year has passed since the capitulation of Germany, and we are naturally asking ourselves: Have these lessons of history been learned or has the ancient adage once again proved true: "History teaches only that history teaches nothing."

It cannot be said that these lessons have been learned by all to the same degree. Insistent fascist agitation is again developing, once again reactionaries are rapturously greeting the speeches of those who would foment war, are casting medals in their honor, are giving them doctor's diplomas as a reward for eloquence, both from ancient European universities and new American colleges. Once again the press of the Stock Exchange and of the Trusts is repeating in every way possible the calls of the important spokesmen of open aggression for a march "to the East." Perhaps new Marlboroughs will succeed where Hitler failed! One cannot help but recall the old French song about martial John Churchill, Duke of Marlborough, which dates from the beginning of the seventeenth century: *"Malbrough s'en va-t-en guerre"* (Marlborough is going away to war).

Of course the reactionaries have a long way to go before they make attempts to resort to a final provocation and to the unleashing of war. But these fomenters of war are meeting their most vexatious opposition from the masses among their own fellow-countrymen, who definitely do not wish a new conflict.

In order to begin an important war in these times there is little preparatory work to be done in setting up strategic bases. No internal work must be done at home such as the Hitlerites in their day did so finally and completely in Germany. "We are on the eve of an anti-labor crusade," Murray, president of the CIO., stated bitterly and publicly to President Truman on the third of June. And he is right: in preparing for more distant crusades the reactionaries are trying to begin with a crusade against their own workers. They must first snuff out the resistance of the working class by anti-labor legislation, which will bind the working class hand and foot.

And at this point they are confronted with great difficulties. For all who really hate Fascism as, for example, Franklin Roosevelt sincerely hated it, know very well that the complete fascization of the internal structure in Germany and her satellites preceded the world conflict.

Nor have the democratic elements, the masses in Britain, in America and other countries, forgotten this lesson of history. In general, the organizers of the third world war are strongly hampered by the fact that the people too well remember the second.

And in those circumstances where reactionary circles of several countries are attracted by a program of world hegemony and robbery, they are falling into manifestly fantastic mental aberrations. As we are seeing, this happens not only with Germans.

I shall cite one of the recent illustrations of this interesting psychological phenomenon.

The matter began in the second half of August 1945 and continues up to the present. In the "big" press of New York, Chicago and San Francisco, and by "big" is meant connected to some degree or other with Wall Street and the trusts, there suddenly appeared the words: "American peace." This expression, even in the original Latin (*Pax Americana*), served as the headline for long newspaper discussions of a political and philosophical nature.

As one can see, these words are an alteration of the famous old Roman expression: *Pax Romana*, that is "Roman peace," "Roman pacification." The authors of the times of the Western Roman Empire understood by these words the cessation of war and the settlement of complete peace on all the expanse of the known world.

It meant the coming of peace because the Romans, by their extensive and uninterrupted campaigns of conquest, had deprived their neighboring peoples of independence and had made of them mute slaves, intimidated half to death. Whichever of the conquered peoples remained submissive enjoyed the "Roman peace." And whoever tried to stir was wiped from the face of the earth. Tacitus and other historians say about the Roman potentates: "Wherever they make a desert, they call it peace" ("*Ubi solitudinem faciunt—pacem appelant*").

This formula of ancient Roman imperialism has continued to allure the beasts of prey of later times who were enthusiastic about it. How often have Karl Haushofer, Goebbels and other fascist corpses shouted of the "German peace" which they would proclaim from the walls of the conquered Kremlin! They also declared that this "German peace" would begin from the end of the year 1941, and would last forever, for the "Hitlerite Thousand Years" (*"Hitlers jahrtausend"*).

Thus when shortly after the atomic bomb was dropped over Hiroshima, in August, in September, October and even later, there suddenly appeared in the Trans-Atlantic newspapers this "American peace." The reader could smell something that was not only old Roman, but was completely close and recent, a thing of yesterday.

And the tone of this publicity resurrected in one's memory how for the noble purpose of maintaining lasting peace, the Romans had promptly converted a foreign land into a desert. Such firmness and speaking the diplomatic language which is fashionable today, "toughness" is even more remarkable because with the imperfect armaments in those far-off ancient times, the business of making a desert was not anything near as easy as it is today, when technical progress is advancing in fabulous seven-league boots.

One more instructive and extremely useful lesson has remained from the second world war. It is the following.

The Soviet people never recognized the "German peace" and it never will recognize a "peace" that is accompanied with threats which comes from any other nations trying to establish their world hegemony.

Throughout its more than thousand-year history Russia never yielded to deceit, although it was at times placed in disadvantageous political positions by means of base flattery and false promises. But no one has ever succeeded in intimidating Russia with threats. Imperialists can most certainly not count on success with this technique against the Soviet Union. At the same time the peace-loving peoples which have just finished with the Hitlerite tyranny, are most certainly not prepared to accept a new yoke, no matter what phrases and what colors are used by the fomenters of the third world war to ornament it.

Today we are observing the fifth anniversary of the beginning of the Great Patriotic War. This is in itself capable of discouraging predictions on the part of anyone expecting favorable results from "toughness" and "sternness" in behavior towards the Soviet people. Hitler was "tough." Himmler was "stern." Where are they? True and lasting peace in our times can only be a peace which is unaccompanied by adjectives added in the name of any state. We need no "Roman peace" in new disguise. Indeed, such a peace is impossible although apparently desirable to someone and the "leadership" of any one country on a world scale is at this moment also completely impossible.

Such are the reflections aroused by the fifth anniversary of the twenty-second of June, 1941.

C.

STALIN'S REPLIES TO WERTH

(*Note: Alexander Werth, correspondent of the London Sunday* Times *in Moscow, sent a series of questions in the form of a letter to Premier Stalin. On September 24, 1946, Stalin's replies to Werth's questions were made public. Read in conjunction with the views expressed by Soviet spokesmen in June 1946 (see Appendices A and B), they represent a renewed assurance by the Russian leader that cooperation between the U.S.S.R. and the United States is still possible.*

It would be well to bear in mind, however, that Stalin is not the sole "boss" of the Soviet Union. The Politburo of the Central Committee of the Communist Party shares responsibility with Stalin and, to an unknown but relative degree, authority. There is indisputable evidence that during the first half of 1946—if not today—the Politburo was split in its ideas about the best tactics for getting along with the United States. A majority believed that a "tough" attitude was necessary; without it, they reasoned, the United States and Great Britain would make continual demands and infringements on spheres of Soviet influence; in short, that the best defense was a truculent offense. A minority, which is said to have included Stalin, believed that the Western democracies would react more favorably to milder, more conciliatory tactics on the part of the Soviet Union and would not take advantage of this Soviet "softness."

This difference of opinion, paralleling somewhat the split in President Truman's cabinet prior to the resignations of Morgenthau, Ickes, and Wallace, still exists. The statements of Premier Stalin which follow indicate that, despite the Soviet press campaign against the United States and despite the attitudes of some Russian officials, the Kremlin still recognizes that the end (peace) is more important than the means (tactics).

Q. *Do you believe in a real danger of a "new war," about which at the present time so much irresponsible talk is being carried on? What steps should be taken for preventing war if such danger exists?*

A. I do not believe in a real danger of a "new war." The noise is being raised about a "new war" mainly by military-political scouts and their few supporters from the ranks of civilian officials.

They need this noise if only (A) to frighten with the

specter of war some naïve politicians from the ranks of their counter-agents and thereby aid their Governments to extract more concessions; (B) to make difficult for some time the reduction of military budgets in their countries; (C) to check demobilization of troops and thereby prevent quick growth of unemployment in their countries.

It is necessary to distinguish sharply between the noise about a "new war," which is being carried on now, and the real danger of a "new war," which does not at present exist.

Q. *Do you think that Great Britain and the United States consciously are forming a "capitalistic encirclement" of the Soviet Union.*

A. I do not think the ruling circles of Great Britain and the United States of America could create a "capitalistic encirclement" of the Soviet Union even if they wanted to do this, which, however, we cannot affirm.

Q. *Speaking in the words Mr. Wallace used in his last speech,* can England, western Europe and the United States be assured that Soviet politics in Germany will not be turned into a weapon of Russian efforts directed against western Europe?*

A. I believe using Germany by the Soviet Union against western Europe and the United States of America is excluded. I believe this is excluded not only because the Soviet Union is bound by a treaty of mutual assistance against German aggression with Great Britain and France, and with the United

* At New York on September 12, 1946.

States of America by the decisions of the Potsdam Conference of the three Great Powers; but also because the politics of using Germany against Western Europe and the United States of America would mean a departure of the Soviet Union from its fundamental national interests.

Speaking briefly, the politics of the Soviet Union in the German question comes down to demilitarization and democratization of Germany. I think that demilitarization and democratization of Germany presents one of the most important guarantees for the establishment of a sound and lasting peace.

Q. *What is your opinion about the accusation that the policies of Communist parties in western Europe are "dictated by Moscow?"*

A. I consider this accusation absurd and to be borrowed from the bankrupt arsenal of Hitler and Goebbels.

Q. *Do you believe in the possibility of a friendly and lasting collaboration of the Soviet Union and western democracy despite the existence of ideological discord, and in friendly competition between the two systems, of which Wallace spoke in his speech?*

A. I do, unconditionally.

Q. *During the sojourn here of the [British] Labor party delegation, you, as I understood it, expressed belief in the possibility of friendly relations between the Soviet Union and Great Britain. What could help in the establishment of*

*these relations, which are so eagerly desired by the broad
masses of the English people?*

A. I really believe in the possibility of friendly relations
between the Soviet Union and Great Britain. Establishment
of such relations would be appreciably helped by strengthening political, trade and cultural relations between these
countries.

*Q. Do you believe that the quickest withdrawal of all
American forces in China is vitally necessary for the future
of peace?*

A. Yes, I do.

*Q. Do you believe that the actual monopoly possession of
the atomic bomb by the United States of America is one of
the principal threats to peace.*

A. I do not believe the atomic bomb to be as serious a
force as certain politicians are inclined to regard it. Atomic
bombs are intended for intimidating weak nerves, but they
cannot decide the outcome of war, since atomic bombs are
by no means sufficient for this purpose. Certainly monopolist
possession of the secret of the atomic bomb does create a
threat, but at least two remedies exist against it:

(A) Monopolist possession of the atomic bomb cannot last
long.

(B) Use of the atomic bomb will be prohibited.

*Q. Do you suppose that with the further advance of the
Soviet Union toward Communism the possibilities for peace-*

ful collaboration with the outside world will not decrease in so far as this concerns the Soviet Union? Is "Communism in one country" possible?

A. I do not doubt that the possibilities for peaceful collaboration not only will not decrease, but can even increase. "Communism in one country" is fully possible, especially in such a country as the Soviet Union.